SPORTS BETTING

D0108570

SPORTS BETTING

A COMPUTER EXPERT'S WINNING SECRETS FOR BETTING ON BASEBALL AND FOOTBALL

JIM JASPER

St. Martin's Press | *New York*

Copyright © 1979 by Jim Jasper
All rights reserved. For information, write:
St. Martin's Press, Inc., 175 Fifth Avenue, New York, N.Y. 10010.
Manufactured in the United States of America

Library of Congress Cataloging in Publication Data

Jasper, Jim.
  Sports betting.

  1. Sports betting. 2. Gambling systems. I. Title.
GV717.J37   796   79–16383
ISBN 0–312–75330–6

Contents

1. | THE JOY OF WINNING   3

2. | THE COMPONENTS OF
BASEBALL BETTING   23

3. | THE BASEBALL SYSTEM:
STARTING A SEASON   36

4. | THE BASEBALL SYSTEM:
THE DAILY ROUTINE   51

5. | BETTING BASEBALL—
THE TOTAL EXPERIENCE   72

6. | PRO FOOTBALL BETTING—
THE COMPONENTS   89

7. | HANDICAPPING THE
NATIONAL FOOTBALL
LEAGUE—THE TEAM   99

8. | HANDICAPPING THE NFL—
CURRENT STRENGTHS
AND WEAKNESSES   116

9. | MY FOOTBALL SYSTEM   130

10. | NEVADA—THE SPORTS
     BETTOR'S PARADISE   147
11. | GAMBLERS—THE WINNERS
     AND THE LOSERS   150
12. | WHAT ARE YOUR PERSONAL
     BEST GAMBLING
     OPPORTUNITIES?   164
13. | DEVELOPING A WINNING
     APPROACH   174
14. | THE WINNING PSYCHOLOGY   186

To the memory of Joe DeBello.

SPORTS BETTING

1 | The Joy of Winning

I paced the floor of my office at Market Facts nervously. It was almost ten fifteen and Georgie hadn't called yet. I had a meeting scheduled in a few minutes to discuss the possibility of acquiring an IBM 360 Model 65 computer. (I was the vice president of Data Processing at the time). It was not likely that my boss would delay the meeting if I told him my bookie hadn't called yet. Georgie and I had missed connections a few times early in the season, and I didn't want to miss betting in the middle of a hot streak. I had just had my fourth consecutive winning week, and after doing my figures for the day's games, it looked as if I would make at least four bets.

I sat down and looked at the notebook in which I kept the day's pitching match-ups, my line on each game, and the running totals for the season. I had won three thousand one hundred and two dollars so far, on an initial bankroll of thirty-two hundred. I had won two hundred eighty bets and lost two hundred and one.

It was ten fifteen. Just as I rose to leave, the phone rang.

"Hello," I said, hoping it was Georgie, and not the president of the company summoning me to the meeting.

"Hello, J., Georgie here," the raspy voice of my bookie replied. I had never met Georgie. But I had a clear mental

3

image of the man who spoke very deliberately, mispronouncing pitchers' names (but never making an error), carefully repeating each bet, the odds, and the amount.

"Hello, Georgie," I said, pencil poised to record the odds on each game.

"Okay . . . here we go." He said exactly the same thing every day.

"Niekro is forty over Jones." He paused, waiting to see if I wanted a bet on that game. ("Forty over Jones" meant the odds on the game were 1.40 to 1, with Niekro the favorite. In baseball betting, there are odds on each game. These odds are called the "line." A "line" of 1.40 to 1.00 would mean that the bettor would risk 140 dollars to win 100 if he were to bet the favored team. This would be called "laying" the odds. If the bettor took the underdog, he would risk 100 dollars to win 140. This is called "taking" the odds.) My line was Niekro 1.42 over Jones. Since I required a 15 percent variation in either direction between my line and the betting line, I did not have a bet, as I had anticipated.

"Nothing there," I said, my standard reply when I did not want to bet a game.

"Okay, Billingham is sixty over Bonham." My line was Billingham 1.93 to 1.00. A bet. I was afraid of that. The Cubs were a jinx team, and I hated laying 1.60 against them. I had a losing record betting Cub games, in spite of my overall success. At least the game was at night, and I wouldn't have to listen to it during work. It always depressed me to listen to Vince Lloyd's dull monotone.

"Gimme Billingham for three dollars," I told him. Three dollars is three hundred dollars in bookie parlance. At 1.60 to 1.00, I had just bet four hundred eighty dollars to win three hundred. In other words, if I lost, I would owe Georgie $480. If I won, he would owe me $300.

"Okay, is everything three dollars?" he asked. I had been betting two sixty a game, but as the winnings mounted, I increased the size of my bets.

"Yes," I answered. I always bet the same amount on each game.

"Okay, Griffin is twenty over Barr." Another bet. My line was Barr 1.13 to 1.00 over Griffin.

"Gimme Barr." I bet three hundred on Barr to win three thirty. If I had bet Griffin, I would have laid 360 to win 300. But the underdog pays ten cents on the dollar less than the favorite. That ten-cent difference is the bookie's edge. If he can get equal action on both sides, he can only win.

Georgie continued to give me the line. There were twelve games, and I bet five of them. The Reds and Billingham over Bonham and the Cubs. The Giants and Barr over Griffin and the Astros. The Yankees and Medich over Lolich and the Tigers, getting 1.30 to 1.00. The Angels and Tanana over the Rangers and the Rookie Phenom, David Clyde, laying 1.20 to 1.00, and the Twins and Goltz over the Orioles and Cuellar.

"Okay, here's what you got," Georgie said, then repeated each bet. "I got eight hundred forty-four dollars your way," he told me when he finished. "I'll see our friend tonight and drop it off."

"Eight hundred forty-four is right," I answered. $844 was my accumulated winnings since the last payoff.

"Okay, talk to you tomorrow," Georgie signed off, ending our conversation. We never chitchatted, never commented on the results, the weather, or anything other than the business we had to transact. "Our friend" was Herschel, the contact between Georgie and myself. We always referred to him as "our friend." Nobody ever told me why.

It was now ten forty. I rushed to my meeting, taking a mental inventory of the day's action. I didn't like betting Billingham or Goltz, but when you have a system you follow it religiously, regardless of your personal preferences. My system had been paying off handsomely, and I wasn't going to change.

I am a Chicagoan, so I could watch the Cub game, and listen to the Tiger, Ranger, and Twins games on my Zenith transoceanic radio. It was going to be an entertaining evening and I looked forward to it all day. The meeting went very well, and the president of the company was convinced by my projections that it was time for us to acquire our own large computer. It was only a question of whether to purchase or lease. A lease was eighteen thousand-plus a month, and the purchase price a little over half a million. We turned that problem over to the company accountant. I was delighted with the results of the meeting, since I had expected a lot more hassle over justifying my figures.

As the day progressed, several of my shareholders dropped by my office to check our bets. (I had sold thirty-two shares, at one hundred dollars each, in the baseball betting venture. I owned six.) Most of the shareholders were co-workers. They all assumed I was using the computer to make my selections. I didn't dissuade them, since they had faith in the computer. Actually, I had used the computer to help me develop my formula, but I did not use it in the day-to-day operation. Larry, a good friend, called in the afternoon. He is an avid baseball fan, and he owned four shares. He and I analyzed the evening's bets, agreeing that we hated Goltz and Billingham. He didn't like betting against Lolich, because the Yankees were lousy against lefties, but I thought the Tigers were awful (my ratings had them as the worst team in the American League at the time), so I didn't mind. Besides, I liked listening to Ernie Harwell, the Tiger announcer. Our analysis was meaningless, since the "system" was doing the picking. But it made us feel better when the system picks made sense to us as handicappers.

At home that evening, we ate dinner, then I played with my three kids, keeping one eye on the clock. The Cub game started at seven. My wife, Charlotte, asked me if I was watching baseball that night. She knew I was, but it gave her the opportunity to voice her disapproval. She liked the money I won, but felt neglected because of the time I spent on gambling, watching games, doing research, and making my calculations.

Game time rolled around, and I set up for the evening. I put the small black-and-white TV on top of the color TV, plugged in my transoceanic next to my reclining chair, got out my portable radio, set a Pepsi on the serving tray, opened a bag of potato chips, and I was ready.

I turned the Cub game on the color TV. Later, when the White Sox got underway, the Cubs would be relegated to the black and white. Though I didn't have a bet on the Sox, they are my first love, and take priority. I would gladly trade my left arm for a White Sox World Championship, something that has not happened in my lifetime. The Tiger game was starting now, too, so I turned on the transoceanic. As soon as Jack Brickhouse announced Bonham versus Billingham, I turned the sound off on the TV. I watched the Cub game while listening to the Yankees and Tigers.

The Reds were easy winners over the Cubs, but the Yankee-Tiger game was a close one, and the Yankees had a 2–0 lead going into the bottom of the ninth inning. With two outs, the Tigers scored a run and had runners at first and second. The hitter singled to right field. Bobby Murcer, the Yankee right fielder, charged the ball. Norm Cash, a slow runner, rounded third for the Tigers. Murcer fired home. "Here comes Cash," boomed Ernie Harwell, the Tiger's fine announcer, "Here comes the throw. *He's out!* The games's over. He's out at the plate."

"Whoopee!" I bellowed, scaring the dog.

By that time, the Angels and Tanana had a commanding 8–1 lead, having bombarded poor David Clyde. The Twins were being routed, and Barr and the Giants had a 3–1 lead in the seventh. It looked good for a 4 and 1 night—over one thousand dollars in winnings. I literally danced into the kitchen to tell Charlotte the good news.

"That's nice," she said without enthusiasm. "Are all the games over?"

"No, but they might as well be, except for the Giants, and they aren't on the radio," I said, meaning I was through with baseball for the time being and would spend the rest of the evening with her. Later, I would check the scores on the news. (The Giants won, Tanana won, the Reds won, and Goltz lost. Plus $1020.)

When I went to bed that night, I had a hard time falling asleep. I couldn't wait for the next day's action. I really felt like I had a tiger by the tail.

Tuesday, I made four bets, winning three for a profit of $520 (the loser was a $1.50 to $1.00 favorite.)

Wednesday, we made nine bets, winning seven, losing two. Profit: $1640.

On Thursday, I upped the bets to $360 a game. When Georgie called Thursday morning, his voice was "business as usual." If he was upset or impressed by my successes, he didn't show it. I bet six games, three favorites. If they all lost, we would lose $2390; if they all won, we'd win $2560. Although it wasn't really all my money, the amount staggered me. I spent the day playing over the possibilities in my head. I imagined listening to winner after winner roll in that night. I figured out the value of a share based on six winners. I couldn't have been higher. The shareholders had been getting word of our successes, and all day they kept popping into my office to look at the blackboard, where I kept the value of a share posted. Their $100 investment had cracked the $300 mark. Many of them had never gambled in their lives. They were thrilled—some of them were really gushing, predicting a final value of at least a thousand. The admiration they expressed was almost as good as the money.

That afternoon, Herschel called. "What are you doing tonight?" he asked.

"Nothing in particular," I replied, "but I do want to listen to the games."

"I have something to discuss with you that would be more appropriately attended to privately," he said mysteriously. I knew better than to probe, though naturally my curiosity was aroused.

"I also have eight dollars that belong to you, so if you could find the time, I'd appreciate it."

"Okay," I assented, "I'll pick you up at six." I knew where dinner would be, an excellent restaurant that was relatively unknown, so a secluded table was still possible. The "eight dollars" he referred to was the eight hundred we had won the previous week.

I called Larry, and asked him if he had any guesses as to the nature of the "private matter." He didn't. My speculations centered around Herschel or Georgie coming up with more money to finance our bets. But that didn't make sense, since both of them had access to my selections, and could bet any amount they chose, without involving me in the profit. Maybe they were unhappy about the rate at which I was increasing the amount of each wager. I finally stopped speculating, and just waited for dinner.

I pulled the car in front of Herschel's apartment building a few minutes before six. He was waiting on the curb. He climbed into the car, smiling broadly.

"Congratulations, James," he said. "I hope your frame of mind reflects the glory of your recent triumphs." The happier Herschel was, the friendlier he felt, the more formal and flowery his already bookish speech became. He peeled eight one-hundred-dollar bills from a roll. "I believe you will find this to be correct, but count it anyway."

"Thank you," I said, accepting the money and quickly counting it.

"Only the beginning, James, only the beginning. The time is rapidly approaching when you will find this paltry sum to be a mere pittance." He laughed with pleasure. One of the real joys of dealing with Herschel was his genuine delight at my successes.

"I hope you're right," I said, nowhere near as confident that things would continue as dramatically as they had up to this point.

"How do you explain it?" he asked.

"I don't know," I shrugged. I always had the uneasy feeling that if I expressed a belief in the permanence of my successes, they would vanish in a puff of smoke. "We're just in a hot streak, I guess."

"Come, come, such modesty does not become you. Never have I seen anyone approach a situation with such directness and singularly systematic aplomb. There are some very anxious people whose money is in extreme jeopardy. Can't you see their faces as the scores come in? Winner, winner, winner. Can you imagine their increasing paranoia?"

Herschel went on in the same vein, painting a picture of the world's bookies huddled fearfully in a corner, cringing every time a score was announced. He chuckled over their dwindling piles of money, their stupidity for not recognizing when they were beat. To him, gambling is a very personal thing. He always plays against an opponent. The psychological aspect of any contest is his meat. He likes beating another person out of his money, and he is damned good at it. I took him on once, and I never will again. Head-to-head gambling is his thing, not mine. He must have a human opponent. My foe is the game, the probabilities, the situation. My pleasure is in developing a system that will win money. I love solving problems, which is why I have risen to the top in the computer field, where problem solving is the key. Baseball betting was the problem I had set out to solve, and the fact that the solution worked was my psychological payoff. Herschel's payoff came when the enemy, in this case the bookie, forked over the cash.

As I drove to the restaurant, he continued his mockery of the bookmakers' mental state as they slowly went bankrupt. Since I had no idea how much of their own money Herschel and Georgie were betting on my picks (Herschel had made it clear that Georgie was on our side), I didn't know how accurate his description of bookie destitution was. I had visions of hundreds of thousands being added to my meager $360 bets. It gave me a feeling of awe. But I knew better than to ask Herschel how much he was betting. His finances were his business. If he wanted me to know, he would have told me.

I wondered if our conversation was leading to the private matter that had necessitated this meeting. "What about the subject you wanted to talk over?" I asked.

"In due time, James, in due time." I felt like a conspirator in a plot to overthrow the nation's bookmakers.

We arrived at the restaurant, and proceeded to have a leisurely meal, discussing the night's action, the food, the sorry state of the world (Herschel's favorite subject, since he is a total pessimist); everything except the "private matter." Herschel should have been a film director. His sense of drama is marvelous. When the coffee arrived, I was ready for anything.

The owner of the restaurant joined us. He was fortyish, mustached, and had the greedy intensity of a self-made businessman. He and Herschel got into a long discussion of the restaurant business. Not only was I anxious to learn the purpose of our meeting, but several of the games we had bet were underway, and I wanted to know how we were doing. After elaborating on the relative merits of soup bars, salad bars, dessert bars, advertising, etc., the owner finally went back to work.

"Well," Herschel said, as he ceremoniously lit a cigar, indicating we were finally going to get down to the nitty-gritty, "has it occurred to you that you are in the midst of something dramatic? Something so remarkable that in many ways it defies belief?" His questions were clearly rhetorical, so I waited patiently for the punch line. "James, what we have here is an event, a happening, if you will, so contrary to the normal course of events, so pregnant with the elements of a fairy tale, that it deserves preservation. It cries out to be shared with the world." He paused, moved closer, smiled, took a leisurely puff from his cigar. "Have you considered writing a book, a diary chronicling this season?"

"No." I was astounded. If I had been given a thousand guesses as to the nature of the "private matter," I wouldn't have come close. First, I did not see why this subject was so sensitive that it could not be handled by phone. The secrecy seemed totally unwarranted. If it had been warranted, certainly writing a book was no way to preserve the secret. Second, I had never even written Herschel a note. He had no idea whether or not I was capable of such a venture.

Finally, things had definitely not reached the point where I was positive I had a permanently winning technique. For one thing, I had won more than my share of the close ones. For another, the season wasn't half over yet; there was plenty of time for the first big losing streak. Although I had to admit that his suggestion was original, I also thought it was ridiculous.

I was very disappointed. I had hoped for something more. But if it hadn't been for Herschel, the whole baseball thing would never have happened. So we discussed the "diary" as if it were a real possibility. I was flattered that he thought my success unique enough for a book. After all, Herschel had been a professional gambler for over twenty years, and he must have been successful many times. I knew of several winning streaks, including his winning twenty-four consecutive football teasers in 1967—a teaser is where the bettor picks three teams to beat the point spread, or to lose to it by less than 12 points—and his dominance in one of the toughest big-money poker games in Chicago. Yet he considered my story worthy of a book. I know now he was aware of some upcoming events of which I was ignorant. But more about that later.

It didn't take long for my interest in the conversation to wane, and I wanted to find out how the games were doing.

"Why don't we continue this discussion in the car, so we can get the scores?" I suggested.

"One thing I like about you, James, you are to the point. I can see you don't think much of my idea, but think about it." With that, we left.

As we approached the car, the adrenaline started flowing and my heart started beating faster, because by now several games were in the late innings. I could be richer or poorer by a substantial amount, and so could my partners. We got in and I started the engine. The radio was tuned to the White Sox, and Harry Caray's raspy, enthusiastic voice filled the car. That was bad. I had bet Billy Champion and the Brewers over Wilbur Wood. Caray, the White Sox announcer, has a "winning" voice, and a "losing" voice. His enthusiasm was a tipoff that the White Sox were ahead. Sure enough, within seconds he gave the score: 6–2 Sox in the seventh.

"That ain't good," I moaned.

"Ah, James, such pessimism. That's only one in six," Herschel replied cheerfully. "Besides, a 1.70 dog can't always be expected to get the job done."

I was about to spin the dial to the Cardinal game, when Caray started giving the scores. It was a disaster. We had the Cards over the Mets. It was 3–1 Mets in the seventh. We had Cincy over the Cubs, 4–3 Cubs, last of the ninth. We had the Yankees over Detroit, 5–2 Tigers top of the eighth. We had K.C. over Boston, 6–0 Boston in the fifth. And we had the Padres over the Phillies, 1–0 Phillies in the fifth. It looked like the bottom had fallen out. My heart sank, and I swore profusely.

"It's not over yet. I predict at least three wins," Herschel said. When he was in a buoyant frame of mind, it took more than a few pinpricks to sink him.

I switched the radio to the Cub game. The Cincinnati crowd was roaring, so something good had happened for the Reds. I wondered how good. After a few seconds, the cheers subsided, and Vince Lloyd, the Cub announcer and a real "rooter," moaned, "Oh, brother, only one out away from a victory, but that Johnny Bench had other ideas. He hit that ball a mile. Well, Lou [Boudreau, his color man], these guys are tough. What a game to lose." My spirits soared. We had pulled that one out. Obviously, Bench had won it with a two-out homer.

"Only the beginning, only the beginning," Herschel chuckled happily.

I spun the dial to the Cardinal game. ". . . and here comes the tying run around third, he'll score, as Brock pulls into second with a double," Jack Buck shouted over the cheers of the crowd. We had tied up the Cardinal game. The disaster was turning into a mild setback.

"I love it!" Herschel exulted. We listened happily as Brock

stole third, scoring when the catcher threw the ball into left field. My sunken heart began climbing back to its normal position.

I turned the dial to the Tiger game. Needless to say, I knew the exact location of every station. "Hiller has finished his warm-ups, and Murcer is ready to step in." Hiller was Detroit's ace reliever, so the Yankees had a rally going. "Top of the ninth, no outs, runners on the corners," Ernie intoned blandly. "Tying run at the plate." Damn, the Yankees were still three down, and Hiller was almost impossible to hit. We listened in disbelief as the Yankees pounded him for three straight hits, the last one a triple, to take a two-run lead.

"Maybe I should write a book, but who would believe it?" I said. Herschel roared with laughter.

I switched back to the White Sox. No miracles there. The score was still 6–2 with the White Sox up in the eighth. Still, the disaster was turning into a break-even proposition. I switched to the Philly game. It is remarkable how many stations you can pick up in the evening. A car radio is even better than the transoceanic. The Philly game was over, and they were doing the Star of the Game show. If I could figure out who they were interviewing, I'd know who won. The interviewer said "Dave, tell us how you got started in baseball." I went through a quick mental check of which team had a Dave. They both did. Cash for the Phils, Winfield for the Padres. We had the Padres. ". . . then I was drafted by the NFL." It was Winfield, who had been a tight end in the Big Ten. We'd pulled that one out, too.

"I don't believe it. The Padres won too," I said. "He's interviewing Winfield, so he must have hit the game winner." Sure enough, the announcer got around to setting up the situation in which Winfield hit a three-run homer in the ninth. From six losers to two winners, two leading, and two losing—all in the space of about five minutes.

"James, there must be some people right now wondering what kind of buzz saw they have run into," Herschel said gleefully. "What I wouldn't give to see them smashing their radios."

Back to the Cardinal game. The Mets went down in the ninth like babies. Hrabosky struck out the last hitter on three pitches. Over to the Tigers. It was finished already. 8–5 Yankees. Four winners. Still 6–2 in the Sox game, and K.C. was down 8–1. It looked like a 4–2 night and another eight-hundred-dollar profit.

"Well, Herschel, I wouldn't have believed it, but that's the quickest turnaround I've seen. Now we just have to get five in the ninth at Comiskey Park, and I *will* write a book." The Brewers did me one better, getting six in the ninth when I was halfway home after dropping Herschel off. By the time I got home, the Sox had gone down in the ninth, and we had won five games. K.C. was down 9–2 at the end of seven when I went to bed. Charlotte was a bit upset that I had spent the evening out when I told her what the "private matter" had turned out to be. "That's all I need, on top of everything else, is for you to be busy writing a dumb book," she complained.

The next morning, as I was getting ready for work, the phone rang. "Hello," I said, expecting a wrong number. Instead, a long, loud laugh boomed over the phone.

"You must be kidding," I said, somehow knowing that K.C. had won. "How did they do it?"

"Four in the eighth, three in the ninth, then they won it in the twelfth," Herschel said exultantly.

"My God, we're rich."

"I am expecting a book to be in my hands, appropriately autographed by the celebrated author, forthwith," Herschel demanded.

Well, it's four years later, but I'm working on it, Herschel, I'm working on it.

The streak continued, though less dramatically, through Sunday. By Monday, payoff day, we had won $3320 for the week, bringing the total for the season to $9621. This made the value of the original $100 share slightly over $400. The shareholders went wild. To my surprise, when Georgie called, he told me he was delivering the money personally. After seventeen years of betting, I was going to meet a bookie face to face for the first time. It made me very nervous. I told him where I worked, and to call me from the lobby phone when he arrived. He said he would get there around one o'clock.

When he called, I told him to stay at the phone, and I would be right down. I described myself as having a mustache and wearing a blue shirt. I hung up and went to the elevator, palms sweating, heart pounding as if I were about to make a speech to a thousand strangers.

When I reached the lobby, I headed straight for the phones, drying my right hand in preparation for a handshake. I spotted Georgie at the phones, and I was surprised by his appearance. He was about sixty, with silver-gray hair, high-blood-pressure red face, and a wry little grin, as if he knew something amusing that no one else knew. He was dressed in a stylish gray sports coat, open shirt, smartly pressed slacks and sparkling brown shoes. He had an enormous diamond ring on his left pinky.

As I approached him, he appraised me in the same way I had sized him up. I wondered if he was surprised. Although I was a vice president of a reasonably large company, I did not wear a jacket or tie, just slacks, a sports shirt, and Hush Puppies.

Instead of shaking hands, he immediately handed me an envelope, saying, "Hello, J. I think this is right."

"Thank you," I said.

"Listen, J., you're doing real good, so I'm gonna start giving you a little bonus." He paused, and I waited excitedly for him to continue. "It's like this, see, for every winner I'll give you a percent. So if you win, say, four dollars on a game, your bonus is four bucks. It isn't much, but if you keep going good, we'll see what else we can do."

"Terrific," I said, quickly calculating that we won about twenty-five games a week, times four dollars, if we bet four hundred (our current bet), which would be one hundred dollars a week for me. And he implied it was only the beginning.

"Listen, J., I gotta run," he said, and left immediately. I was overwhelmed. This was it. A bookie actually paying *me* to bet with him! I had never even heard of such a thing. It was the ultimate compliment. I almost didn't need an elevator to get to the sixteenth floor. I had the most money I had ever held in my hands in the white envelope, and the promise of much, much more to come. What a joy it was to win!

The story has a happy ending, too. By season's end, a $100 share was worth $579. My bonus was raised to 2 percent (it doesn't seem like much, but from 1974 to 1976 I received $28,000 in bonuses alone). My personal winnings in 1974 exceeded $10,000. Not only was I a hero to my seventeen shareholders, but I had ten grand in green money to show for my efforts, and six months of having a ball. I'd had the time of my life. Even the acquisition of the computer turned out well, and my company gave me a substantial bonus.

Oh, the joy of winning. That is the point of this book. It is possible to win, and it's fun to win. Sports betting is a wise investment if you do it right. In this book I will introduce you to some winning techniques, as well as illustrating the approaches to developing winning techniques. I will discuss techniques for money management and developing a winning psychology.

But the most important point of this book is to show that gambling to win is a positive, vitality-producing activity that is a joy unto itself. The hours you spend betting will be as happy and fulfilling as anyone could hope for. A group of sociologists I used to work with did a study of happiness. They discovered that people with the highest overall happiness quotient were those who had hobbies they loved. Well, betting is as sensible a hobby as golf, carpentry, or stamp collecting, and less expensive, provided you are doing it to win. Even if you don't develop the skills needed to win, and lose a few hundred a year, that's still fine if you enjoy it. Is it any more foolish to spend a few hundred on your hobby if it is betting than if it is fishing? If it turns you on, it is well worth the money. And if you apply yourself, you can make it profitable. It can be done. I've done it. In fact, it is how I make a living now.

It isn't easy. I wasn't born a winner. In fact, I didn't make my first bet until I was nine years old. I bet my brother a million dollars I could hold my breath longer than he could, and I won. We had just moved to a new flat, and we were sitting on the kitchen floor, waiting for the movers to arrive with the furniture. There were a bunch of flies buzzing around, so I gave him a chance to get even by betting another million on who could catch the most flies. My fly-catching technique was superior to his, and I won again. Out of boredom, we kept betting on one silly thing or another. When the furniture finally showed up, my brother owed me forty-seven million. My chances of collecting being relatively slim, I settled for a nickel.

I started gambling in earnest in 1958, betting horses, football, gin rummy, poker, and anything else I could. But I was a loser. I loved the anxiety, so I made bets just for the sake of the action. I had a reasonable grasp of how to win, but I really didn't care if I won or lost, I just wanted to bet, bet, bet.

Fortunately, I also loved figuring things out, so I learned a lot while I was losing, and made a lot of good contacts in the gambling world. Then, in 1964, I became a computer programmer. As soon as I had mastered the skills required to get what I wanted out of a computer, I started using it to analyze various gambling situations. I developed programs for blackjack, poker, football, and numerous programs for horse racing in the years between 1964 and 1969. But, because I was still a loser psychologically, I made enough nonsystematic bets, and bets on systems that hadn't been thoroughly tested, to outweigh my winnings on the good systems.

By the summer of 1969, I had a considerable arsenal of

winning techniques. And then I found a key to my own psychology that turned me into a winner. My boss at that time was a good friend of mine, and he knew I was a losing gambler. He also knew I was using the computer to try and beat the bookies. One day, he accused me of wasting my time, stating flatly, "You can't beat the bookies." Although I hadn't done it, I knew it could be done. So I challenged him to book all my bets on horses and sports.

At first, my losing psychology prevailed, and I continued mixing in enough off-the-wall bets with my good bets to lose. He laughed every time I paid him, rubbing it in. It got so bad, he even went to the track with me, so he could benefit from my losing instead of me feeding the parimutuel machines.

I became really determined to beat him, and for the first time in my life, gambled strictly to win. I increased my horse-racing efforts, writing several computer programs, checking each system the computer came up with thoroughly. I began making system bets only, and stopped handicapping. And I started winning. And I kept winning. My boss decided to book my football bets, too. (We both had access to the book-maker's football line.) So I stopped playing every football game on TV, and bet only my computer selections. And I beat him badly at football.

Now I was laughing when he paid me, and I discovered something. Winning was fun. Much more fun than losing had been. I became as addicted to winning as I had been to just betting. But I still had a few lessons to learn.

My boss was a good poker player, and played in a "friendly" game regularly. One afternoon, he invited me to join the game. I accepted, and that evening I went in rubbing my hands, figuring I had become a winner, and this was another golden opportunity. I got destroyed. So I read a book, and tried again. I got destroyed again. I wrote a poker program, memorized all kinds of odds, practiced memoriz-ing cards, and went back again. I broke even. I played weekly for eight months, and gradually started to lose again. I can't play poker. I learned that wanting to win is not enough. You also have to know how. In addition to an understanding of the odds, you have to have good instincts, to be able to "read" the other players. I didn't have it. So I stopped playing poker, and concentrated on the games I was good at.

Eventually, my boss was convinced you *could* beat the horses and sports (especially after signing his paycheck over to me for a month straight) and resigned as my bookie. And suddenly my winning incentive was less. I had worked hard enough to have produced so many techniques that I showed a consistent profit, but nowhere near the maximum possible result. So, for a few years, I stumbled along winning a few thousand a year.

Then, in 1974, I sold shares in my gambling. I had the reputation at work, and among my friends, of really knowing sports, and everyone knew about my many successful computer programs. So, when the opportunity came along to bet baseball, and my finances were down (I'd just bought a house), I decided to "incorporate." I was surprised how easy it was to sell shares. I stopped at thirty-two, limiting any one person to six shares. But I could have sold a hundred easily. The results, as I have described previously, were spectacular. I *really* wanted to win for my shareholders. Bad bets with other people's money were out of the question. I knew having shareholders would work, because of my terrific record betting horses whenever a beginner I took to the track entrusted me with his money. I am not only a natural showoff, I also have a strong sense of responsibility. I couldn't disappoint the people who had shown faith in me.

As silly as it seems, I still needed to trick myself into wanting to win. Having succeeded in doing that, I had one more lesson to learn—how to manage money. During the sensational baseball season of 1974, I increased my bets too quickly, and was reluctant to reduce them; as a result, a late-season losing streak cut too heavily into the profits. Conversely, when betting horses I tended to bet the same amount for too long—another cause of reduced profits. I have also been a little too quick to spend the winnings. So, in 1975, I did a computer analysis of money management, based on an anticipated profit rate, probabilities of losing streaks, and bankroll size. Now I manage my money strictly on a formula basis. How much I bet, when to take a profit, and even when to abandon a betting technique is totally systematic. This has helped me to make the most of my capital and winning techniques. (Chapter 13 explains money management in detail).

I can hear some people saying, "He's taking all the fun out of it. What about Monday night football? How can I pass it up? Or go to the track and not bet every race?" The answer is simple. If you are gambling for recreation, bet small. If you are betting seriously, to win, bet serious amounts. But make sure you know when you are doing which. I still bet almost every televised baseball or football game. But I only bet twenty bucks a game if none of my systems is applicable. (Herschel now lets me bet twenty, and he adds his eighty, to make it one hundred.) So it basically costs me a dollar for the entertainment. (If you bet twenty, you lose twenty-two when you lose, win twenty when you win. Since you should win half the time, you should lose two dollars for every two bets you make, or one dollar per twenty-dollar bet.) Although this method doesn't produce the anxiety I used to crave, it helps me win. One must recognize one's weaknesses, and find a nondestructive way to deal with them. I have a dangerous craving for action, so I give in to it in a small way, and protect my profits. If you want to make a small wager, I'm sure you can find a friend willing to bet.

These are the lessons I had to learn to become a winner. Some may apply to you, some not. But before you can become a winner, you will surely have to be aware of your weaknesses, and find a way to conquer them. This book not only describes winning systems, it also has many suggestions for recognizing and conquering the losing psychology. When you put it all together, it spells m-o-n-e-y.

The next few chapters give the details of betting baseball to win. When you read them, you will see that a lot of hard work went into the development of my baseball system. I enjoyed every minute of it. You will also see that a reasonable amount of effort is required to use the system. This fact is important. People feel guilty, whether they know it or not, about getting something for nothing. Winning at baseball will not be getting something for nothing. You will earn it— systematic betting requires work. You are working now, reading this book. Place a value on your time, to protect yourself from feeling guilty about winning. Guilt produces losing. Remember, you are earning your future winnings right now.

2 | The Components of Baseball Betting

The first step in approaching any gambling opportunity is to understand the betting environment. This requires answering several questions:

1. What are the betting rules?
2. What is the bookie's take, or the house percentage?
3. Who is the competition; who are you really betting against?
4. Is the game "honest"?
5. What information is available to you?
6. Is there information available to the competition that isn't available to you?
7. Do you like the game?
8. What special abilities do you bring to the situation?

Having answered these questions, you can decide whether or not you think you can eventually win, and analyze the problem of learning to win. In this chapter, we will look at the above questions and analyze baseball from a betting perspective. In the next two, I will explain my system.

1. What are the betting rules?

Baseball betting is (with occasional exceptions) a matter of picking the winning team. There is no "point spread." But there are odds. When you bet the favorite, you "lay" the odds. For example, if a team is an 8–5 favorite, you must lay (i.e., risk) eight dollars to win five. When you bet the underdog, you take the odds. However, you don't take the same odds as you would have laid. In an 8–5 game, you would take 7–5 odds if you bet the underdog. This is called a "twenty-cent" line, meaning the bookie's edge is twenty cents on the dollar; 1.60–1.00 versus 1.40–1.00, or 8–5 versus 7–5. This twenty-cent line is prevalent in the East and Las Vegas. In Chicago, a "ten-cent" line is still available. So, if a favorite is 8–5, you get 7 1/2–5 on the underdog (1.60–1.00 versus 1.50–1.00). But if the line is 9–5 or greater, the ten-cent line becomes a twenty-cent line (9–5 versus 8–5). At odds of greater than 2–1, most bookies use a forty-cent line (2.40–1.00 versus 2.00–1.00). Occasionally, there will be a "run" line, in which case you add runs to the underdog's score. For example, if a team is a two-run favorite, you must give two runs if you bet the favorite, but you only get 1 1/2 runs if you bet the dog.

When you bet baseball, you may specify that "pitchers must go." This means you don't have a bet unless the pitchers for whom the line was quoted are the starting pitchers. I always specify "pitchers must go," because if an unlisted pitcher starts the bookie adjusts the odds *after* the game. Otherwise, you get the odds at the time you bet, even if they change later.

For example, let's say Tom Seaver is scheduled to pitch against Don Sutton, and is a 1.40 favorite. If I were to bet the game, I would specify Seaver over Sutton, and I would lay $1.40, no matter what the odds wound up at. (The odds change frequently. In fact, if my bet were large enough, it could cause the odds to change). Now, let's say for some reason Seaver didn't start, but Bill Bonham did. There is a big difference between a Tom Seaver and Bill Bonham, and I certainly wouldn't want to bet on Bonham—especially since the bookie can adjust the odds however he chooses, which of course gives him a big edge. So, always specify "listed pitchers" or "pitchers must go."

One last betting rule: if a game is an official game, but is called because of darkness, curfew, power failure, etc., your bet counts and the score at the time the game is called is considered the final score, even though the game will be completed later. If it is tied when called, it is a "no bet," regardless of who wins when it is resumed.

There are also various gimmick bets, the most popular being the "over-under." In this bet, a total-run figure is specified; for example, eight runs. You can wager that the total runs scored by both teams will be over or under eight runs. If you bet over-unders, you must lay 11–10 or 6–5, depending on the size of your bookie's heart. (If you have access to weather conditions, particularly the direction and strength of the wind relative to the layout of the ball park, over-unders can be beautiful; otherwise, they are tough.) The other gimmick bets are too stacked in the bookie's favor to bother with. (Such things as picking a player to get three hits and getting odds of 8–5, which is ridiculous, or picking a player to hit a home run and getting 8–5, which is also ridiculous, particularly since they "bar" Wrigley Field.)

2. What is the bookie's take?

The bookie's take, or percentage, varies. On a twenty-cent line it varies from 4.5 percent at 6–5 to 3.1 percent at 2–1. On the ten-cent line it varies from 2.4 percent at 6–5 to 1.8 percent at 1.70 to 1.00. The forty-cent line of 2.40 to 2.00 is also 4.5 percent. Obviously, it is worth finding a ten-cent line. Betting into a ten-cent line, the average take is about 2.2 percent. Betting into the twenty-cent line, the average take is about 3.8%. The "average" line is 7–5, or 1.40 to 1.00. Let's say the White Sox were a 7–5 favorite over Milwaukee. That means the "true" odds, without a bookie's take, should be

1.30 to 1.00 (splitting the difference between the 1.40 to 1.00 you would lay on the favorite and the 1.20 you would take on the dog). The ten-cent line, in this case, would be 1.35 on the White Sox, 1.25 if you took Milwaukee. Let's say you made one hundred such bets on the White Sox, winning fifty-five, at $100 each you would win $5500 and lose $6300 against the twenty-cent line, $6075 against the ten-cent line. If you had chosen Milwaukee and won forty-five and lost fifty-five, you would lose $5500 and win $5400 against the twenty-cent line and $5625 against the ten-cent line. Quite a difference. If you bet 500 games a year, it is worth the equivalent of eight extra winners to be betting into the ten-cent line instead of the twenty-cent line.

In my opinion, the bookie take on baseball is quite small, particularly compared to most other betting opportunities where the bettor has the choice and can introduce skill into his selections. The take would be horrendous for a "luck" game, like dice, or flipping coins. But an average take of under 4 percent is not unbeatable—especially when you consider, for example, that the horse racing parimutuel take is 16 to 20 percent.

So far, baseball qualifies as a potential betting opportunity.

3. Who is the competition?

Although you make your bet against a bookie, he is merely a broker, and *not* the competition. The competition is the professional linemaker, and the baseball-betting public. The professional linemaker is a knowledgeable, first-rate baseball expert. He doesn't make the odds according to what he thinks they should be, but rather according to how he thinks the public will bet. His goal is to attract the bettors equally to both teams. When he is wrong, and more people bet one team than the other, the bookie will change the odds in order to discourage betting on the team that has been getting the most action. For example, let's say the line on Tanana versus Perry is 7–5, with Tanana the favorite. If a bookie takes in several bets on Tanana, he could lose money, unless he can attract some bets on Perry. So, he will raise the line to 7 1/2–5, hoping to get enough Perry action to balance his books, so that he will win either way. If the bettors keep betting Tanana, he will go to 8–5. If he starts getting too much money bet on Perry, he will move the line down again. So, for the most part, the betting public is the competition.

Who is the betting public? Mostly people with money, mostly serious fans, and some professional gamblers. Baseball bettors are a pretty tough group to beat, probably the most knowledgeable gamblers you will encounter. They have weaknesses, though not very big ones: long memories, prejudices, loyalties to particular teams, bad gambling psychology. Overall, they tend to bet right, and the line will move in the direction of the winner more often than not. So I try to bet against the opening line unless I want to bet against a pitcher or team the public has been betting lately. I would rather compete with the linemaker's guess than what turns out to be the bettor's true evaluation of the game. (My bets are so frequently in the direction of the "steam"—the "smart" money—that Georgie calls me instantly when he gets the line, so he can get our action in before the line has time to move.

If the bookie's take were bigger, or if I had to bet against the closing line, baseball would be much harder to beat. But by making the linemaker my opponent, I have an edge. I'm trying to figure the odds on the game; he's making odds on the bettors. Obviously, if I do a good job, I'm going to come closer to the true odds than he does, which means I can beat him. And so can you.

4. Is the game "honest"?

The evidence says yes. There has not been a scandal since the 1919 Black Sox. They threw the World Series to the Cincinnati Reds, or at least some of them did. Since then, there hasn't even been a hint of any hanky-panky. Bookies trust baseball, or they wouldn't take bets as large as they do. (I know of "outs" (bookies) where you can get down as much as ten big ones, $10,000, on a single game.) The players are well paid. And it would be a hard game to fix absolutely. No matter who you got to, he might not successfully throw the game. I suppose a home-plate umpire or a pitcher would have a good shot at it, but they still might not be able to do it. So, in my book, baseball rates an A-plus in the honesty area.

5. What information is available to you?

The statistics available on baseball are the most complete, and the most easily and cheaply obtained, of any sports betting opportunity. The box scores of every game, with each individual's performance, are published in most newspapers. Summaries of team and individual statistics are available in many Sunday editions, as well as the *St. Louis Sporting News,* a fine sports newspaper. Magazines are published every spring containing career statistics for all rostered major leaguers. There is ample information available to enable a bettor to make informed wagers.

A shortage of "How to Bet Baseball" type books makes it difficult to learn from other people's research and experiences. Almost nothing exists on the predictive nature of baseball statistics. There are also very few "public handicappers" like there are for horses and football. So it was necessary for me to start from scratch to develop a baseball betting technique. You are luckier, since you have this book to get you started.

If you are a baseball fan, you know that individual performance tends to vary a relatively small amount from year to year. This is an important fact to keep in mind. A .300 hitter is not likely to hit under .270 or over .330, and that is only a 3-percent difference in each direction. So, not only is there a lot of information available on baseball, but it is very valuable as predictive information.

6. Is there information available to the competition that isn't available to you?

Because baseball is played daily, it does not produce much "hidden" information, such as injuries, dissension, etc., which are common to football and basketball. You can usually find out about injuries by looking at the box scores and reading the sports pages. Disciplinary benchings are almost always part of the sports news. So it is pretty easy to know who is going to play and who isn't. In addition, you are allowed to specify that the most important player, the pitcher, must play, or you have no bet. Weather, a big factor in football, doesn't matter much, except to "over-unders."

The nice thing about baseball is that you can get more information than the competition if you are diligent. You don't need access to any insider's grapevine; all you have to do is listen to the radio, especially if you are in an area where you can pick up a lot of out-of-town stations. In Chicago, I can listen to fourteen of the twenty-six major-league teams. I frequently learn about injuries as they happen because I'm listening to a game.

Also, you can increase the information edge you have on the competition by keeping statistics yourself that are not ordinarily published. This can dramatically improve your edge in making selections. You can know practically anything you want about baseball, if you are willing to put forth the effort. For instance, I know each team's run-scoring average and won-lost record against left- versus right-handed starters, the exact earned-run average of their relief pitching, the runs scored per game in every park in the majors, etc. When it comes to baseball, if anyone has an information edge on me, he's earned it.

7. Do you like the game?

This is very important. As I've said previously, it requires work to win. Even playing something as simple as a slot machine requires pulling a handle. (When they put in slots that spun automatically, people didn't play them. It proves my point that people want to "earn" their money, even if it just requires pulling a handle.) If you like the game, the work involved will be fun. To me, this is the big plus—you can earn your money through hard work, and enjoy every minute of it. If you don't take any other advice from this book, remember this: Bet on games you love, that you can get really wrapped up in. It is the *sine qua non* of betting.

I love baseball; it is my passion. I have loved the game since I was nine years old and my parents sent me to Comiskey Park and Wrigley Field every day instead of hiring a baby-sitter. Taffy Wright, a potbellied outfielder who could hit, was my hero. Bob Elson, the White Sox announcer, was another hero. I used to listen to him do the ticker-tape broadcasts of the road games, not understanding the esoteric idioms, like a "grounder to short, Appling gobbles it up and fires to first," or "there's a high pop fly to short center, a can of corn, Tucker is under it and takes it for the out." At first, it was like listening to a foreign language, but Elson's silky voice and glibness made it musical and fascinating. And he was always spouting numbers as if they explained everything. I had to learn how to speak and understand this magical language. I listened constantly, read the newspaper for the first time in my life, devouring the sports pages. I went to the library and read every book they had, fiction or nonfiction, on the subject of baseball.

The statistics became my obsession. I was probably the only kid in my fifth-grade class who understood decimals, having figured them out from an article on computing earned-run averages. When most kids were buying comic books, I bought baseball magazines. I used to ride my bike two miles to a candy store that sold individual baseball cards for a penny. By the time I was sixteen, I had over ten thousand baseball cards, which represented a lot of skipped lunches. During the winters, I would memorize each player's RBIs, home runs, batting average, etc.

To amuse myself, I invented a baseball simulation game

based on the statistics, and played the entire 1953 baseball season, in advance, on our kitchen table. My family thought I was nuts, but I loved it. That experience proved the predictive nature of baseball statistics to me, since my pennant and World Series winners did, indeed, win in 1953.

Do I like the game? You bet I do!

8. What special abilities do you bring to the situation?

Knowledge, of course, is one kind of special ability you can bring to a game. But knowledge can be acquired. Understanding how a game works is important, and harder to acquire. If a game has statistical components, and most do, a talent or knack with numbers helps. Memory is important to some games, as is general intelligence. The ability to be an observant spectator, catching lots of details, is helpful in sports betting. An analytical mind is always beneficial. "Card sense" is a tremendous ability. I wish I had it. The ability to "read" people—the individual players, the teams, even the betting public—helps in some games. Being a hard worker always contributes to success. The list goes on and on.

What special abilities do I personally bring to the baseball betting situation? First, I know baseball thoroughly. Second, I understand it, in my opinion, better than the majority of the managers and general managers who run the game. Third, baseball betting is very susceptible to statistical analysis, and I am definitely a numbers type. Fourth, I like the game enough to work very hard at it. Fifth, I have a very analytical mind, which I have had to develop in the computer business. Sixth, I know how to use a computer, which has turned out to be very instrumental in my success with baseball. I feel I bring a strong set of special abilities to the baseball betting situation.

Having looked at all the above questions, the last question is, can I beat the game? Let's look at the pluses and minuses. The biggest minus is the toughness of the competition.

This is partly overcome if you bet against the opening line, but it is still the largest single obstacle. Another big minus, particularly if you don't have access to the ten-cent line, is the bookie's take. It is not an insignificant percentage, but it is not too high to beat. The last personal minus is that I am a White Sox fan, which could be dangerous if it led me into making heart bets. These are my shortcomings as a baseball bettor—everybody has a few.

The pluses are numerous. First, the betting rules favor the player, since he can pick the teams and pitchers he wants against a "stationary" target. (Unlike horse betting, where the odds are changed on you after you bet.) Second, it is an honest game, so you can't get cheated out of your money. Third, there is a plethora of accurate, reliable information. Fourth, with diligence you can get an information edge on the competition. Fifth, I have an intense love of the game. And finally, I have learned enough about myself to overcome the loser instinct, and by a considerable margin. The conclusion? For me, baseball clearly represents an opportunity to win.

Once I decided I could beat baseball and found the outlet for my wagers, I turned my attention to analyzing baseball as a betting proposition. Since baseball is bet using an odds line, my goal had to be the creation of a more accurate odds line than the linemakers'.

The first approach I looked at was a baseball simulation program on the computer. In this approach, I would have the computer "play" each game one thousand times, using its results to establish the probability, or odds, of each team winning. I would have fed in the statistics on each individual; and, using a random number generator to obtain the result of each batter's trip to the plate against each pitcher, I could play the game a batter at a time one thousand times. There were two drawbacks to this technique, unfortunately. (I still think that if this technique were feasible, the amount of money you could win would be phenomenal.) The first drawback, which would be surmountable with enough hard work, is the lack of statistics on such things as runner speed, where hitters hit the ball most, how often a runner can move up a base on an out, etc., all of which are essential to a simulation program. I could have guessed, and probably with a high degree of accuracy. But the second, more important drawback *was* insurmountable at the time, so I didn't bother. The big problem turned out to be the cost of the computer time to simulate each game. I figured it would take the IBM 360/65 about one minute per game. One minute of time on the 360/65 was going for about $20 at that time, so it would have cost $240 a day to predict every game. Too much. (The cost of computer time has been coming down dramatically in the past few years. Pretty soon, this approach will cost less than a buck or two a game. When that day comes, I expect to do even better on baseball). I probably could have stolen the computer time, but there was no way I was going to jeopardize my livelihood—besides, my conscience would have bothered me. I could justify my research efforts, since they took a trivial amount of computer time, and I always ran them when the computer was not otherwise occupied.

Having abandoned the simulation approach, I thought hard about baseball. First, baseball is an individual sport, requiring less teamwork than any other team sport you can bet on. And almost all individual baseball skills are measured statistically. There are only a few that aren't, such as hit and run ability, moving runners from second to third, hitting the cutoff man, and backing up plays. But if you are an avid fan, you know which players excel in these categories, and which players are terrible.

Unless a player changes teams, his "intangibles" show up in his teammates' statistics. The runner he moves from second to third scores more runs. If he always hits the cutoff man, his pitcher's earned-run average will be lower. The intangibles produce or prevent runs.

So, except for trades, the individual statistics tell the story. Now the question arises: out of the myriad statistics, which ones matter?

For starting pitchers, earned-run average tells the story. Strikeouts, walks, wins, and losses are interesting, but how many runs does he allow every nine innings? The ERA tells me what to expect—it is the predictive statistic for starting pitchers.

But pitchers give up unearned runs. These are the fault of his defense. For example, if there are two outs, runners on first and third, and the shortstop makes an error on a ground ball, and the runner scores from third, that is an unearned run because it wasn't the pitcher's fault. If any more runs were to score in that inning, they too would be unearned, since there would have been three outs if the shortstop hadn't erred. The number of unearned runs charged to a specific pitcher is, in my opinion, non-predictable. The number of unearned runs given up by a team *is* a predictable statistic.

Finally, starting pitchers often do not pitch the full nine innings. Relief pitching is an important consideration. A team's relief pitching has become a major factor in its ability to win. This leads to two more predictive statistics. First, the number of innings each pitcher averages per start. Second, a team's overall earned-run average for relief pitching.

The above statistics are all it takes to produce a defensive prediction for every starting pitcher.

On offense, each player contributes to his team's run scoring ability, and he contributes in two ways: by scoring runs, and by driving runs in. The predictable statistics for hitters are runs scored per plate appearance, and runs batted in per plate appearance. All other statistics, including the glamour statistics of batting average and home runs, are non-predictive of a player's contribution to the production of runs.

The final predictor is a general one: What is the home team advantage? This is not available, so I took the results of five seasons and determined that the home team wins 6 games and loses 5, on the average.

Having decided all the predictable variables, I was ready to predict which team would win each game, and by how much. But baseball is a game in which you bet by odds, not a "run spread." Before I was ready to bet, I needed a way to convert my run predictions to an odds line.

I used the computer to get the magic conversion formula. I keypunched the score of every game played for two years. I then wrote a program to tell me what the value of each tenth of a run in difference was.* I expected to have a complicated conversion chart, but, to my amazement, the results were almost linear. All I had to do to get a line was divide the run difference by two, and add the result to 1.00. That gave me the line. For example, if my prediction was White Sox 4.42, Twins 4.02, the difference (.40) divided by two is .20, plus 1.00 = 1.20. My line would be the White Sox 1.20 to 1.00 (6–5) over the Twins.

The computer had given me the final ingredient in my initial approach. I had chosen all the predictable statistics, and I'd determined how to turn a prediction into a line. All that was left was to establish a procedure for making predictions, and then put it to the test.

*The procedure I used was as follows: I arranged all the scores in storage, in two arrays. Each 1/10 of a run represented an increase of 1/42, since 4.2 was the average number of runs scored. So, as I increased the difference of the two arrays by 1/10 of a run, I randomly added one run to 1 out of every 42 entries in the "superior" array. Then I compared every score in the superior array to every score in the "inferior" array, giving a win when it was higher, a loss when it was lower, a 1/2 win and 1/2 loss when they tied. I then divided the losses by 100, and the wins by the result, giving me the line for 1/10 of a run superiority. I repeated the process, again adding a run randomly to 1 out of 42 entries, compared the arrays again, and got the line for a 2/10 difference. (I allowed repeats in my random number generator, since the increased runs certainly, in reality, would not distribute at a run per game.)

3 | The Baseball System: Starting a Season

Before we get into the details of my baseball system, let's talk about the advantages of system play versus handicapping, and vice versa.

System play represents the scientific approach to betting. Handicapping is the artistic approach. The advantages of the scientific approach are:

1. You eliminate emotional factors from your betting selections.
2. Your selection technique is constant, and you can measure a scientific system's performance on past results.
3. You can handle a large number of events.
4. You can use a scientific system designed by someone else, saving you the time and effort required to develop your "artistic" ability.
5. You can't force a system to make a selection just because you want to make a bet.

The disadvantages of system play are:

1. No system can take every fact into consideration.
2. Systems can be boring to use.
3. You don't get that creative "thrill" in making system bets.
4. Systematic betting requires hard work.

The advantages of handicapping are:
1. It is fun.
2. You can take absolutely everything into account.
3. You can use your mind, which is more powerful than any computer.
4. If you are a true expert, you know things that can't be put into a formula.

The disadvantages of handicapping are:
1. Your emotions can beat you.
2. The money pressures can cloud your judgment.
3. In any high volume betting situation (like baseball), there is too much to think about if you evaluate every game. You must limit your handicapping to a few games a day. This forces you to pass up too many betting opportunities.

Each person will have to decide for himself whether to be a systems bettor or a handicapper. Most people should be systems players, because they don't have the discipline to handicap successfully. But there is no better "investor" than the first-rate handicapper. Perhaps reading this chapter will help you choose your favorite approach.

My baseball system consists of two basic parts, the predictors at the start of the season, and the daily procedures for using and updating the predictors once the season is underway. This chapter is devoted to computing the predictors before they start playing—based on the statistics from the previous season. The next chapter will describe the daily procedures during the season. For those of you who hate statistics, skip to Chapter 5, where (in addition to baseball handicapping) I discuss some shortcuts to baseball betting that don't produce quite as much action or profit, but which will make money with not too much effort.

Getting started every year requires the most effort you will have to put forth at any given time. The necessary raw statistics can be found in the year end wrap-up issue of *The Sporting News* or in the *Who's Who of Baseball*. In addition, an electronic calculator is absolutely necessary for this process. If the calculator has the "memory" feature, it will cut down substantially on the amount of work you have to do. You can get one with "memory" for under $30, at the time of this writing. If you use one of the new "programmable" calculators, your work load will be further reduced. These are much more expensive (and more difficult to master) but they are also a lot of fun. However, I only recommend them for the real "figure" buffs. I use a calculator with memory, and it takes me about ten hours to do the calculations required to start the season, and about 18 hours a week thereafter.

Rather than insert the formulas into the narrative, I have put them all at the end of the chapter. Each formula is given in a step-by-step format and in algebraic terms. There is also an example, plus a test case, with the right answer. Work the test case to make sure you get the right answer to verify that you understand the formulas. You don't want to bet your money on a mistake.

The first calculation you must make (Example 1) is to compute the average number of runs scored each game, for both the American and National leagues. This figure allows you to compare each starting pitcher to the average.

The second calculation produces each team's unearned-run percentage (Example 2). This figure is used to adjust each pitcher's ERA to produce the total (unearned and earned) runs he will allow per nine-inning game.

The next calculation needed is each team's bullpen rating (Example 3). This is the most difficult rating to produce accurately, since pitchers are shuttled in and out of the bullpen so frequently. Relief pitchers are the most likely to be traded, released, or shipped to the minors. So every year, the guys in the bullpen change more than anything else. I used to have a very complicated formula for the bullpen rating, and it was still my most inaccurate figure. So I studied bullpens thoroughly, and discovered a simple fact. The two best relievers in each team were the only ones that really mattered. The others generally pitched only when the games were already lost, or in "garbage" games (the 12–11, or 18-inning games, etc.) which are totally unpredictable. The "ace" of the bullpen is by far the most important man, because he will be summoned when the game is close—either when the score is tied, or with his team ahead by one or two runs. The ace is usually easy to identify, since he will have the most saves.

The second-best guy in the bullpen usually comes in when the game is close in the early innings, or when the team is behind by a run or two late in the game. The reliever with the most appearances (other than the ace) is usually the second-best reliever. Once you have decided who the two top men in the bullpen are, the formula is easy to follow. If you don't follow baseball closely enough to identify the "ace" and his backup man, and it isn't evident from the statistics, ask a friend who is a baseball nut to help you. Otherwise, try calling the sports department of your local newspaper. They love to show off their expertise.

The next calculation is an important one—the total defensive rating for starting pitchers (Example 5). This rating is made up of three components. A pitcher's ERA (earned-run average), his team's defensive ability (unearned-run percentage), and the bullpen rating. Example 5 applies to pitchers who started in at least two thirds of their appearances, and pitched at least seventy-five innings.

The result of the formula in Example 5 is the rating for the pitcher, the percentage of the "average runs per game" that the pitcher would allow against the mythical "average" team. This is the figure that is used every time he pitches, to compute the correct odds on the game. More about that in the next chapter.

Many starting pitchers change teams, and require adjusting. Example 4 gives the formula for adjusting a pitcher's statistics when he changes teams. This formula is based on a computer analysis that showed how much easier or harder it is to score runs in each ball park, and to figure out what happens to a pitcher when he goes from a good team to a bad team or vice versa. For example, everyone knows Wrigley Field in Chicago is a hitter's paradise and a pitcher's nightmare. Pitcher after pitcher has left mediocrity with the Cubs to become a winner elsewhere. But how much difference does this variable make? My analysis shows that 17 percent more runs will cross the plate per team in Wrigley Field than they would in Shea Stadium. Table 1 shows the difference for every park in baseball.

The formula in Example 4 also adjusts for the abilities of the new team versus the old. A pitcher's ERA goes down when he moves to a better team because good teams execute the defensive intangibles better. My computer analysis shows that a team that wins ten games more than another will cut a pitcher's ERA by about .10 on the average.

I do not have formulas for rookie pitchers or relief pitchers. I do not attempt to make a line on these pitchers, because I have no facts, or because I have insufficient facts to make an accurate line. I do have techniques for betting these games when I cannot make a line, and they will be discussed in Chapter 5.

Next, we must calculate each team's offensive rating, or run-scoring ability (Example 6). The first step is to determine each team's starting lineup against left- and right-handed pitching. If every player played for the team the preceding year, you are ready to perform the calculations in Example 6. If a player in the starting lineup played for a different team the preceding year, it is necessary to adjust his statistics. Rookies in a starting lineup are another problem. It is impossible to use minor-league statistics, since they do not accurately predict major-league performance. What I did was take every rookie who broke into the starting lineup and compare his run production to the veteran who would have played if the rookie hadn't. The results showed that the rookies did almost identically, on the average. As a result, in setting each team's starting lineup, I always use a veteran in every position, even though I know a rookie has won the job. (Note: If the rookie is starting due to trades or injuries, use a veteran who is available, not the traded or injured player.)

The formula for computing each player's offensive value is based on my opinion that run production (runs scored and runs batted in) per plate appearance is the only true measure of a player's contribution. Batting average doesn't do it. Remember the Harvey Kuenn for Rockey Colavito deal? It destroyed the Indians because Kuenn's high batting average just didn't produce the runs that Colavito's power did. But power doesn't tell the whole story, either. Joe Rudi doesn't have tremendous power, but he produces runs. Reggie Jackson has power and speed, so he is one of the biggest run producers in baseball. (He is also one of the most valuable. His team is in the playoffs and World Series regularly.)

We now have an offensive rating based on individual statistics, which is a big advantage, since it allows us to accurately adjust our rating to account for injuries, just by substituting the replacement's statistics for the injured player's statistics.

We are now ready to start the season. We have a defensive rating (percent of average runs allowed) for most starting pitchers. We also have an offensive rating (runs scored per game) for each team against left- or right-handed pitchers. Play ball! It gets my adrenaline flowing just to think about it.

Example 1. Average Runs Per Game, Each League.

Following are the games played and runs scored for every team in the majors in 1977 (all statistics can be obtained from *The Sporting News,* or other baseball publications):

AMERICAN LEAGUE			NATIONAL LEAGUE		
TEAM	GAMES	RUNS	TEAM	GAMES	RUNS
MINN	161	867	PHIL	162	847
BOS	161	859	CIN	162	802

continued

continued

AMERICAN LEAGUE			NATIONAL LEAGUE		
NY	162	831	PITT	162	734
CHI	162	844	ST L	162	737
KC	162	822	CHI	162	692
TEX	162	767	LA	162	769
CLE	161	676	MONT	162	665
DET	162	714	HOU	162	680
BALT	161	719	ATL	162	678
MIL	162	639	SF	162	673
SEA	162	624	SD	162	692
CAL	162	675	NY	162	587
TOR	161	605			
OAK	161	605			
TOTALS	**2262**	**10247**		**1944**	**8556**

To get the average number of runs scored, divide total runs for each league by total games. In the American League, you divide 10247 by 2262, getting 4.53 as the American League average.

Stated algebraically, let:

G = sum of all games played (2262 for the American League)

R = sum of all runs (10247 for the American League)

MR = average runs per game

Then R/G = MR or, for the American League, 10247/2262 = 4.53

The correct average for the National League is 4.40.

Example 2. Unearned run percentage, each team.

Here are the statistics we needed to make this calculation (in 1977—you'll have to update for the current season):

TEAM	INNINGS PITCHED	RUNS ALLOWED	ERA
White Sox	1445	771	4.25
Cubs	1468	739	4.01

First, we must compute the total run average per nine innings for the White Sox. To do this, multiply total runs allowed, 771, by 9; then divide the result (6939) by the number of innings pitched (1445), giving 4.80. Next, subtract the ERA (4.25) from the total run average, (4.80), giving .55, the number of unearned runs per nine innings. Divide .55 by 4.25 and you get the unearned run percent for the White Sox, .129.

Stated algebraically, let

T = total runs allowed (771 for Sox)
I = innings pitched (1445 for Sox)
E = ERA (4.25 for Sox)
A = average runs per nine innings
D = difference between ERA and total average runs
U = unearned run percent.

Then, our formula is:

$T \times 9/I = A$
$A - E = D$
$D/E = U$
or, in our example:
$771 \times 9/1445 = 4.80$
$4.80 - 4.25 = .55$
$.55/4.25 = .129$
The Cubs' unearned run percent is .129.

Example 3. Bullpen rating, each team. Here are the statistics needed to compute a bullpen rating for the Cubs and the Dodgers:

NAME	ERA	SAVES	
Sutter	1.35	31	ACE
Hernandez	3.03	4	second best
Cubs team ERA: 4.01			

NAME	ERA	SAVES	
Hough	3.30	22	ACE
Garman	2.71	12	second best
Dodgers team ERA: 3.22			

Because the ace is most likely to appear in a close game, he counts for 35 percent of the bullpen rating. The second best reliever counts for 25 percent. The other 40 percent will perform approximately .75 runs per game worse than the team average. So, we multiply Sutter's ERA (1.35) by .35, giving .4725. Then we multiply Hernandez's ERA (3.03) by .25, giving .7575. The Cubs team ERA, 4.01 plus .75, is multiplied by .40, giving 1.904. These products are then added (.4725 + .7575 + 1.904), giving 3.13, which is the Cubs bullpen rating.

Stated algebraically, let:

A = Ace's ERA
B = second-best's ERA
E = team's ERA
R = bullpen rating

Our formula is:

$$(A \times .35) + (B \times .25) + ([E + .75] \times .40) = R$$
or, in our example:

$(1.35 \times .35) + (3.03 \times .25) + ([4.01 + .75] \times .40) = 3.13$
The correct answer for the Dodgers is 3.42.

Example 4. Adjustments to ERA's based on team changes.

There are two factors that affect a pitcher's ERA when he changes teams: the home park, where he will pitch half his games, and the ability of the team playing behind him. So, our adjustment when a pitcher changes requires two steps: the first to normalize for the home-field difference, the second to account for the difference in ability.

In order to adjust for the home park, use Table 1 (page 46). First, locate the pitcher's former team in Column 1. Multiply the number in Column 1 by his earned-run average. This adjusts his ERA to what it would have been in the mythical "average" park. Then, locate his new team, and multiply his "average" ERA by the figure in Column 2. This adjusts his ERA for his new park.

Now, to adjust for the difference in team ability, subtract the number of wins his new team had the previous year from the number his old team had. If his new team is better, subtract that number from the decimals in his ERA. (If it was 10 games difference, subtract .10). If worse, add the difference to his ERA.

Here are the statistics we need to compute the adjusted ERA for Bill Bonham (at the end of 1977), who switched from the Cubs to the Reds, and Woody Fryman, who switched from the Reds to the Cubs.

PLAYER	ERA	TEAM	WON
BONHAM	4.35	CIN	88
FRYMAN	5.40	CHI	81

First, we multiply Bonham's ERA (4.35) by .87, the figure for the Cubs in Column 1 of Table 1, giving 3.78. Then, we multiply 3.78 by 1.02, the number for Cincinnati in Column

2 of Table 1, giving 3.86. Then, we subtract the number of wins the Cubs had (81) from the number of wins for the Reds (88), giving 7. We multiply 7 by .01, giving .07, which we subtract from 3.86, giving 3.79, Bill Bonham's adjusted ERA.

Stated algebraically, let

E = pitcher's ERA (4.35 for Bonham)
R = old team's Column 1 figure from Table 1 (.87 for Cubs)
N = new team's Column 2 figure from Table 1 (1.02 for Reds)
W = new team's wins (88 for Reds)
L = old team's wins (81 for Cubs)
A = adjusted ERA

Then our formula is:

$$([E \times R] \times N) - ([W-L] \times .01) = A$$
or, in our example,
$$([4.35 \times .87] \times 1.02) - ([88-81] \times .01) = 3.79$$

Fryman's adjusted ERA is 6.05

TABLE 1. PARK ADJUSTMENT FACTORS

A.L. TEAM	COLUMN 1	COLUMN 2
Orioles	1.06	.95
Red Sox	.85	1.17
Angels	1.08	.93
White Sox	1.01	.99
Indians	1.01	.99
Tigers	.94	1.07
Royals	1.00	1.00
Brewers	1.03	.97
Twins	.97	1.03
Yankees	1.01	.99
As	1.07	.94

continued

continued TABLE 1. PARK ADJUSTMENT FACTORS

A.L. TEAM	COLUMN 1	COLUMN 2
Mariners	1.00	1.00
Rangers	1.02	.98
Blue Jays	.96	1.05

N.L. TEAM	COLUMN 1	COLUMN 2
Braves	.86	1.16
Cubs	.87	1.13
Reds	.98	1.02
Astros	1.08	.93
Dodgers	1.02	.98
Expos	1.01	.99
Mets	1.04	.96
Phillies	1.01	.99
Pirates	.98	1.02
Cardinals	1.05	.95
Padres	1.07	.94
Giants	.96	1.04

Example 5. Calculating ratings for each starting pitcher.

Here we want to give each pitcher a rating that can be used to predict the number of runs he will allow against any given team. The mythical "average" pitcher would have a rating of 1.00, meaning each team's offensive rating would be multiplied by 1.00 to obtain the predicted number of runs. (The average pitcher would allow each team its average number of runs per game.) Obviously, better than average pitchers will have ratings lower than 1.00, and bad pitchers will rate above 1.00.

Here are the statistics for Francisco Barrios of the White Sox (in 1977):

Games   33
Innings   231
ERA   4.13
The White Sox unearned percent is .129.
The White Sox bullpen rating is 3.71.
    The American League average runs per game is 4.53.

First, we must determine how many innings Barrios will pitch, and how many the bullpen will pitch. To do this, we divide innings pitched (231) by games (33), giving 7.00. So, Barrios will pitch 7 innings, the bullpen 2. Next, we divide 7 by 9, giving .77. So Barrios will pitch 77 percent of the game, the bullpen 23 percent. We then multiply Barrios's ERA (4.13) by .77, giving 3.18. We multiply the bullpen rating (3.71) by .23, giving .85. Adding 3.18 to .85 gives 4.03, the number of earned runs that will be scored, on the average, when Barrios pitches. We increase this by the unearned run percent for the White Sox by multiplying by 1.129, giving 4.55; to get Barrios's final rating, we divide 4.55 by 4.53, the league average, giving 1.004.
    Stated algebraically, let

$$E = \text{ERA} \qquad\qquad (4.13 \text{ for Barrios})$$
$$G = \text{Games} \qquad\quad\; (33 \text{ for Barrios})$$
$$I = \text{Innings pitched} \quad (231 \text{ for Barrios})$$
$$U = \text{unearned run percent} \quad (.129 \text{ for White Sox})$$
$$B = \text{bullpen rating} \quad\;\; (3.71 \text{ for White Sox})$$
$$L = \text{league average runs} \quad (4.53 \text{ for AL})$$
$$R = \text{rating}$$

Then, our formula is

$$\left[\left(\frac{\frac{I}{G}}{9} \times E \right) + B \left(1.00 - \frac{\frac{I}{G}}{9} \right) \right] \times \frac{(U + 1)}{L} = R$$

or, in our example:

$$[(231/33/9 \times 4.13) + 3.71 \times (1-(231/33/9)]] \times (.129+1)/4.53$$
$$= 1.004$$

Here are the statistics for Ken Kravec of the White Sox. His rating is .994:

GAMES	26
INNINGS	167
ERA	4.10

Note: If a pitcher has changed teams, you must adjust his ERA (as in Example 4) before applying this formula.

Example 6. Computing a team's run-scoring ability, or offensive rating.

The first step is to figure out who will be playing against lefties and righties for each team. If you don't know, wait until the season starts, when you can see who is playing. If any players are used who played for a different team the previous year, their rating must be adjusted, using Table 1. If a rookie is being used (anyone who didn't bat one hundred times the previous year), use the rating for the veteran he has displaced.

Here are the 1977 statistics for the New York Yankees:

NAME	AB	R	RBI	RATING
MUNSON	595	85	100	.621
CHAMBLISS	600	90	90	.600
RANDOLPH	551	91	40	.475
DENT	477	54	49	.431
NETTLES	589	99	107	.699
PINIELLA	339	47	45	.542
RIVERS	505	79	69	.586

continued

continued

NAME	AB	R	RBI	RATING
JACKSON	525	93	110	.773
SPENCER*	470	56	69	.531
JOHNSON**	142	24	31	.774

*Plays against righties
**Plays against lefties

To compute an individual's rating, add together his runs scored and runs batted in, and divide by his at bats, then multiply by 2. For Chris Chambliss, 90 runs, plus 90 RBI, divided by 600 AB, gives .300 times 2 or .600. Chambliss will produce .600 runs per game.

Jim Spencer played for the White Sox in 1977. His rating with the White Sox was .531. To adjust his rating for his new park, use Table 1. First, multiply by Column 1 for his old team, the White Sox (1.01), then multiply by Column 2 for the Yankees, his new team (.99), giving .531. (You don't have to adjust for team ability with hitters.)

Once each individual rating has been computed, add together the ratings for the nine players who will play against each type of pitching. For the Yankees, this produces 5.26 against righties and 5.50 against lefties. The Yankees' offensive rating is 5.26 against righties, meaning they should average 5.26 runs a game against average pitching.

The algebraic formula for a player's rating is:

$$([R + RBI]/AB) \times 2$$

The team rating is the sum of the nine players. In the National League, I use a pitcher's lifetime batting statistics, or give a pitcher a rating of .300 if his lifetime at bats are under 100. You may have problems getting this information. Some years I manage to find it by buying enough baseball books, other years I just use .300 for all pitchers. This is not a problem in the American League, where pitchers don't bat.

4 | The Baseball System: The Daily Routine

We are now ready for the day-to-day business of making a line on every game. For the first few games of the season, this is relatively simple, since we use only the previous year's statistics (See Chapter 3). But in order to make a line as the season progresses, we must incorporate the current year's performances into our ratings. This involves keeping certain statistics, and applying formulas to update pitcher and team ratings. I will give the reasoning behind the update formulas here. The examples and algebraic formulas are at the end of the chapter.

For the purpose of updating statistics, I keep a chart on each team and on each starting pitcher. At the beginning of each season, I enter my basic team statistics (unearned run percentage, bullpen rating, and team offensive rating) at the top of the appropriate team rating chart (see Figure 2). I also enter my starting pitcher ratings (defensive ratings) at the top of the ratings chart that I maintain for each starting pitcher on each team (see Figure 1). Then I compute the predicted number of runs scored for each team (Example 1), assuming the game was played on a neutral field. Next, I convert the predicted run difference into the "line," based on my discovery that one run is worth fifty cents on the line (Example 2). Then I must modify the line to take into account the home team advantage (Example 3). The home team wins about 56% of the time, a figure which has been increasing lately. (My theory is that increased attendance helps the home team, and major-league attendance has been steadily increasing.)

Now, I have my line on each game. I will bet any game where the bookie's opening line varies from my line by at least 15 percent. Example 4 shows the formula for determining if a game is bettable.

The next part of my routine is the really fun part—watching and listening to as many games as I can. But I don't do it just for fun. For the purposes of my system, I also find out about injuries, managerial decisions (such as the benching of a regular, or deciding to platoon, or putting a starter in the bullpen, etc.) I can also usually find out who the starting pitchers will be the next night. (This information can be useful, since the newspapers, and sometimes even the bookmakers, can be wrong). You can also pick up lots of useful information from the sportscasters and by observation, which can be used to make non-system (or instinctive) bets —but more about that in Chapter 5.

The morning after the games have been played, I buy a newspaper, and check the box scores for missing regulars. If a regular didn't play, I make a note of it, and I record who was substituted for him. Unless I know a player is injured, I assume that one missed game is meaningless. But if a player is out two games in a row, I assume he is injured and will not play the next game. When a player is injured, I adjust his team's offensive rating by substituting the replacement's rating for the regular's rating.

Next, I read the newspaper account of each game, mostly for injury information, but also out of curiosity. I like to know how I won or lost each game.

Then comes the tedious part. For each game, I must record the pertinent statistics (see Figure 1). First, I record the starting pitcher's performance. I keep a separate sheet

FIGURE 1

STARTING PITCHER CALCULATIONS—Tom Seaver RT
Cincinnati (for 1978)

Pre-season Defensive Rating (Example 5, Ch. 3) = .673

1 DATE	2 TEAM	3 LINE	4 SCORE	5 IN	6 R	7 TOTAL IN.	8 TOTAL R	9 RATING
4/6	Hou	−1.85	W 11-9	3	5			.703
4/11	SF	−2.60	L 2-3	7	2	10	7	.703
4/16	Hou*	−1.45	L 3-4†	6	2	16	9	.703
4/21	SF*	−1.70	L 0-3†	7	1	23	10	.698

*road game
†indicates which team I bet (I bet against Seaver on 4/16 and 4/21)

for every starting pitcher, with one line of information for
every start he makes. This line contains the date (1), the
team (2) he pitched against, the line on the game (3),
whether I bet on or against him, the score (4), the number of innings he pitched (5), the number of earned runs
he allowed (6), his total innings pitched to date (7), his
total runs allowed to date (8), and his updated rating (9).
(See Example 5.)

In updating a pitcher's rating, each start counts for roughly
.4 percent of the new rating. I do not allow ratings to change
by more than 3 percent (say, from .965 to .935) because
extreme performances distort the ratings.

FIGURE 2

TEAM STATISTICS—CINCINATTI (for the 1978 season)

Pre-season calculations:
Unearned run percentage .070 (Ex. 2, Ch. 4)
Bullpen rating 4.24 (Ex. 3, Ch. 4)
Team offensive rating (Ex. 6, Ch. 4): right 5.08
left 5.08

	① L	② R	③ WL	④ WR	⑤ E	⑥ U	⑦ BI	⑧ BR	⑨ F
Pre-season									.070
Morgan out	59	111	8-7	11-7	146	12	113.1	43	
Bench out		116		12-7	147		118.1	44	
Morgan In	63		8-8		152		120.1	44	7.1

L (1) Runs vs. LT
R (2) Runs vs. RT
WL (3) Won-lost vs. lefties
WR (4) Won-lost vs. righties
E (5) Earned runs allowed to date
U (6) Unearned runs allowed to date
BI (7) Bullpen innings pitched
BR (8) Bullpen earned runs
F (9) Current unearned run percentage
LT (10) Current offensive rating vs. lefties

FIGURE 2

TEAM STATISTICS—CINCINATTI (for the 1978 season)

	⑩ LT	⑪ RT	⑫ B	⑬ L+	⑭ R+	⑮ H	⑯ A	⑰ ON	⑱ AG
Pre-season	5.08	5.08	4.24						
Morgan out				−3.2	+.2	−1.9	−1.1	+2.45	+2.55
Bench out					+1.2		− .1		
Morgan In	4.88	5.31	3.90	−4.4			−1.3		+3.65

RT (11) Current offensive rating vs. righties
B (12) Current bullpen rating
L+ (13) Money won/lost if you always
    bet them vs. LT
R+ (14) Money won/lost if you always
    bet them vs. RT
H (15) Money on home games
A (16) Money on road games
ON (17) Results betting on them
AG (18) Results betting against
    them

Next, I have a statistics page for each team (in Figure 2 I provide a few entries from my daily sheet for 1977). On this I record total runs scored to date against lefties (1) and righties (2), won-lost record against lefties (3) and righties (4) (the starting—not winning or losing—pitcher is the one who determines whether a game is recorded in the lefty or righty columns), earned runs allowed to date (5); unearned runs allowed to date (6); innings pitched by the bullpen (7); earned runs allowed by the bullpen (8); my updated unearned run percentage for the team (9); my updated offensive rating for the team against lefties (10); righties (11); and my updated bullpen rating for the team (12). For my own curiosity (and in order to keep track of my progress) I also calculate where I would stand if I always bet on the team against lefties (13), righties (14), at home (15), and away (16). Finally, I calculate how I have done betting on (17) and against (18) the team to date. In the far right margin, I keep notes relevant to my current wager (substitutions, injuries, etc.).

As the season progresses, it is necessary to update each team's offensive and defensive ratings before I can bet on a particular game. I perform these updates every Monday and Friday morning. I count each game played as one percent of the overall rating. After ten games, therefore, the current year's statistics will constitute 10 percent of the ratings, and the prior year 90 percent; after 100 games, the current year will constitute 100 percent of the ratings, and the prior year will be meaningless.

The biweekly updates differ from the formulas used to start the season, since actual performances are used, rather than projections. For the offensive ratings, I do not use the individual performances but the actual team performance. This is more a matter of expediency than accuracy. It is unreasonable to keep and compute the individual statistics on every player, so I just use the team's run scoring to get the offensive rating. This gives you a very close approximation. You would need a computer to keep up with updating each player, and even then it would take ten or more hours a day.

Example 6 gives the formula for the update of each team's offensive rating.

In the formula for updating bullpen ratings (Example 7) and unearned-run percent (Example 8), I simply use a team's actual performance, again counting each game as one percent of the total rating.

Once the season is underway, the formula for predicting the number of runs scored by each team changes (Example 9). You will notice that the formula doubles the importance of each pitcher's last three games. This was an important discovery—that pitchers go on streaks, pitching well or poorly in spurts, and doubling the importance of their most recent performances in predicting what they will do.

After predicting the number of runs for each team, you use the same formulas (Examples 2, 3, and 4) in determining which games are bettable.

Computing each day's line takes about one hour per day. Recording the statistics takes another hour a day. The updates on Mondays and Fridays take about two hours each. So the total time expenditure is 18 hours a week. Needless to say, many of you will not wish to spend that kind of time on betting baseball. For those people, the next chapter presents other possible approaches to the situation. These methods are not as reliable, but, intelligently applied, they can provide you with a lot of fun and some profit, with a more reasonable investment of time.

However, for those of you who enjoy fooling with numbers, the system is tremendously rewarding. You get an awfully smug feeling as you watch the numbers predict the collapse of a team (like the 1974 Tigers), then collect your winnings when the predicted downfall takes place. It's also fun to rate a pitcher tops (Ron Guidry, 1978) and watch him win game after game; or to see a team add a player with a dynamite rating—like Larry Hisle (Brewers, 1978)—and astound the baseball world, but not your figures.

That's not to say you will win every bet. But I have been using this system for five years, and my profit every year has been between 8 and 10 percent. I make between five hundred and six hundred system bets a year, so it isn't just luck, it works. And my system can work for you if you're willing to put in the necessary time.

Example 1.   Predicting each team's runs for a given game, against a given pitcher.

Here are the relevant figures for predicting two particular games in 1978:

TEAM	PITCHER	PITCHER RATING	TEAM OFFENSIVE RATING*
YANKS	GUIDRY	.672	5.47
SOX	WOOD	1.071	5.07
REDS	BONHAM	.914	5.07
DODGERS	HOOTON	.734	4.99

*Remember that the lineup (and the offensive rating) varies according to the starting pitcher (lefty or righty)

For each team, multiply their offensive rating by the opposing pitcher's rating. For the Yankees, 5.47 by 1.071, giving 5.86, the number of runs predicted for the Yankees. For the White Sox, 5.07 by .672, giving 3.41. We predict that, on a neutral field, Guidry will beat Wood 5.86 to 3.41. Remember, the pitcher's rating is intended to show the percentage of a team's average run production he will allow. Wood is a below-average pitcher, so he will increase a team's run production. Guidry is above average, so he will decrease a team's run production.

The formula is: pitcher rating × team rating = runs.

If Bonham were to pitch against Hooton, we would predict a score of Dodgers 4.56 Reds 3.72.

Example 2.   Converting run predictions to a line.

Given the above run predictions, to convert to a line, subtract the lower number from the higher, divide by two, and add one. The team with the higher number is obviously the favorite. For the Yankees and White Sox, we subtract 3.41 from 5.86, giving 2.45. Divide that by two and you get 1.225. Add one and you get 2.225. On a neutral field, Guidry would be a 2.225 to 1 favorite over Wilbur Wood. Let:

$$H = \text{higher predicted runs (5.86 for Yanks)}$$
$$L = \text{lower predicted runs (3.41 for Sox)}$$

Then our formula is:

$$\frac{H - L}{2} + 1 = \text{line}$$

$$\frac{5.86 - 3.41}{2} + 1 = 2.225$$

The line on the Dodger-Reds is 1.42 in favor of the Dodgers.

Example 3. Adjusting for the home-team advantage.
The final step in creating our line is to adjust it for the home-team advantage. Let's assume the Yankees are the home team in the above example. There is a very complicated formula for adjusting lines based on odds (which involves eight calculations), but it takes too long, so I have constructed a table (Table 2) that has the necessary calculations built in. Just look down the first column to locate the odds on the favorite. If the home team is the favorite, look in the second column for the amount to add to the odds. If the visiting team is the favorite, look in the third column for the amount to subtract from the odds. If the amount subtracted reduces the visiting team's favoritism below 1.0 to 1, then the home team becomes the favorite by the amount of the difference. (If a visiting team would have been a 1.15 to 1 favorite on a neutral field, the home team becomes a 1.05 to 1 favorite). The Yankees are a 2.225 favorite in our exam-

ple. Locating 2.20 to 2.39 in column one, column two says add
.35, giving 2.585, our final line on the game.

TABLE 2

LINE	ADD	SUBTRACT
1.0 to 1.19	.20	.20
1.2 to 1.39	.22	.24
1.4 to 1.59	.24	.27
1.6 to 1.79	.26	.30
1.8 to 1.99	.29	.34
2.00 to 2.19	.32	.38
2.2 to 2.39	.35	.45
2.4 up	.40	.55

Here are several examples:

Visitor favored 1.385 becomes visitor favored 1.145
Visitor favored 1.015 becomes home favored 1.185
Home favored 1.650 becomes home favored 1.910

Example 4. Determining if a game is bettable.

I only bet if the bookie's line varies by 15 percent from my
line. So, I multiply my line by .15, then subtract the result
from my line, and add the result to my line. This gives me
the upper and lower limits of the line. If the bookie line falls
within my limits, I don't bet. If it is below my lower limit, I
bet the favorite. If it is above my upper limit, I bet the
underdog. In our example, my line was Guidry 2.585 over
Wood. Fifteen percent of 2.585 is .387. Subtracting .387 from
2.585 gives 2.198. I could bet Guidry at odds of 2.15 to 1 or less,
but not at 2.20 or more. Adding .387 to 2.585 gives 2.972. I
could bet Wood at plus 3 to 1, but not at plus 2.95 to 1 or less.
If my line were 1.05 on a game, 15 percent would be .158. A
.158 variation from my line would be 1.108 to 1 against the

team I made the favorite. I would have to get +1.15 to 1 to bet a team I made a 1.05 favorite.

The formula would be:

My line − (my line × .15) = lower limit
My line + (my line × .15) = upper limit

Bet the favorite if the bookie's line is less than the lower limit. Bet the underdog if the bookie's line is greater than the upper limit.

Examples:

MY LINE	LOWER LIMIT	UPPER LIMIT
1.0 to 1.0	+1.15	+1.15 (Bet either team at +1.15)
1.30 to 1.0	−1.05	+1.50
1.60 to 1.0	−1.35	+1.85

Once the season has started, you must apply the following updates (Examples 5–9) before you can determine your wager (Examples 2–4).

Example 5. Updating each pitcher's rating for each start.

To update each pitcher's rating, I have constructed four tables (Table 3) to save calculating time. First, find the grid that matches a pitcher's current rating. Next, find the row matching the number of innings he pitched. Then, find the column matching the number of *earned* runs he allowed. The figure in that box is added or subtracted to the pitcher's rating. For example, suppose Tom Seaver's rating is .684, and he pitches 7 2/3 innings, allowing three earned runs. His rating is under .750, so we look under the grid headed "rating under .750." The entry for 7–7 2/3 innings, 3 runs, is +.010. So Tom Seaver's updated rating would be .684 + .010, or .694.

Here are some samples:

OLD RATING	INNINGS PITCHED	RUNS	NEW (UPDATED) RATING
.675	3	5	.705
.894	9	2	.879
.986	12	3	.981
1.153	4	2	1.148
1.200	0	3	1.230

Example 6. Updating a team's offensive rating.

I keep track of a team's run production against right- and left-handed pitching, and a team has a rating for both kinds of pitching once the season starts. Let's assume the following team statistics:

TEAM	GAMES VS. LEFT	GAMES VS. RIGHT	RUNS VS. LEFT	RUNS VS. RIGHT	RATING VS. LEFT	RATING VS. RIGHT
CUBS	14	26	47	111	4.26	4.26
YANKS	20	22	93	91	5.47	5.21

First, I get a team's total rating, by dividing total runs (47 + 111 = 158 for the Cubs) by games played (14 + 26 = 40), giving 3.95. Then I get their rating against lefties by dividing runs versus lefties (47) by games played against lefties (14), giving 3.36. I count overall rating as 80 percent, rating against lefties as 20 percent, so I multiply overall rating (3.95) by .8, and lefty rating (3.36) by .2, and add the results, (3.16 + .67) giving 3.83. That is the Cubs' rating versus lefties so far this year. Remember each game played is worth one percent; the Cubs have played 40 games, so this year's rating is worth .40, and I should multiply 3.83 (this year's lefty rating) by .40, giving 1.532, and last year's lefty rating (4.26)

TABLE 3
RATING UNDER .750

RUNS

Innings	0	1	2	3	4	5	6	7
0-2/3	.000	+.020	+.030	+.030	+.030	+.030	+.030	+.030
1-1 2/3	.000	+.015	+.025	+.030	+.030	+.030	+.030	+.030
2-2 2/3	.000	+.010	+.020	+.030	+.030	+.030	+.030	+.030
3-3 2/3	-.005	+.005	+.015	+.030	+.030	+.030	+.030	+.030
4-4 2/3	-.010	.000	+.010	+.025	+.030	+.030	+.030	+.030
5-5 2/3	-.010	.000	+.005	+.020	+.030	+.030	+.030	+.030
6-6 2/3	-.015	-.005	.000	+.015	+.025	+.030	+.030	+.030
7-7 2/3	-.015	-.005	.000	+.010	+.020	+.025	+.030	+.030
8-8 2/3	-.020	-.010	-.005	+.005	+.015	+.020	+.025	+.030
9-9+	-.025	-.020	-.010	.000	+.010	+.015	+.020	+.030

RATING .750 TO .899

RUNS

Innings	0	1	2	3	4	5	6	7
0-2/3	.000	+.015	+.030	+.030	+.030	+.030	+.030	+.030
1-1 2/3	−.005	+.010	+.030	+.030	+.030	+.030	+.030	+.030
2-2 2/3	−.005	.000	+.020	+.030	+.030	+.030	+.030	+.030
3-3 2/3	−.010	.000	+.010	+.025	+.030	+.030	+.030	+.030
4-4 2/3	−.015	−.005	+.005	+.015	+.025	+.030	+.030	+.030
5-5 2/3	−.015	−.010	.000	+.010	+.020	+.030	+.030	+.030
6-6 2/3	−.020	−.015	−.005	+.005	+.015	+.025	+.030	+.030
7-7 2/3	−.020	−.015	−.010	.000	+.010	+.020	+.025	+.030
8-8 2/3	−.025	−.020	−.010	.000	+.010	+.015	+.020	+.030
9-9+	−.030	−.020	−.015	−.005	+.005	+.015	+.020	+.030

RATING .900 TO 1.099

RUNS

Innings	0	1	2	3	4	5	6	7
0-2/3	.000	+.015	+.030	+.030	+.030	+.030	+.030	+.030
1-1 2/3	−.005	+.005	+.025	+.030	+.030	+.030	+.030	+.030
2-2 2/3	−.005	.000	+.020	+.030	+.030	+.030	+.030	+.030
3-3 2/3	−.010	.000	+.015	+.025	+.030	+.030	+.030	+.030
4-4 2/3	−.015	−.005	+.005	+.020	+.025	+.030	+.030	+.030
5-5 2/3	−.020	−.010	.000	+.010	+.020	+.025	+.030	+.030
6-6 2/3	−.025	−.015	−.005	+.005	+.010	+.020	+.025	+.030
7-7 2/3	−.025	−.020	−.010	.000	+.005	+.015	+.020	+.030
8-8 2/3	−.030	−.020	−.010	.000	+.005	+.015	+.020	+.030
9-9+	−.030	−.025	−.015	−.005	.000	+.010	+.015	+.030

RATING 1,100 AND ABOVE

RUNS

Innings	0	1	2	3	4	5	6	7
0-2/3	.000	+.010	+.020	+.030	+.030	+.030	+.030	+.030
1-1 2/3	-.005	.000	+.015	+.030	+.030	+.030	+.030	+.030
2-2 2/3	-.010	.000	+.005	+.025	+.030	+.030	+.030	+.030
3-3 2/3	-.015	-.005	.000	+.020	+.025	+.030	+.030	+.030
4-4 2/3	-.020	-.010	-.005	+.015	+.020	+.025	+.030	+.030
5-5 2/3	-.025	-.015	-.010	+.005	+.010	+.020	+.025	+.030
6-6 2/3	-.025	-.020	-.010	.000	+.005	+.015	+.020	+.030
7-7 2/3	-.030	-.020	-.015	-.005	.000	+.010	+.020	+.030
8-8 2/3	-.030	-.025	-.015	-.005	.000	+.010	+.020	+.025
9-9+	-.030	-.025	-.020	-.010	-.005	+.010	+.015	+.025

by .60, giving 2.556. Adding the two results (1.532 + 2.556) gives 4.09, the updated offensive rating for the Cubs against lefties. To get their rating against righties, divide 111 by 26, giving 4.27. 4.27 times .20 gives .85, plus 3.16 (.8 × 3.95) gives 4.01, this year's rating so far. 4.01 times .40 is 1.604, 4.26 times .60 is 2.556. 1.604 plus 2.556 is 4.16, the Cubs' updated rating vs. righties.

Let:

RL   = runs versus left
RR   = runs versus right
GL   = games versus left
GR   = games versus right
L   = lefty rating, previous year
R   = righty rating, previous year.

Then our formula is:

Step One: $(RL+RR)/(GL+GR)$ = C (Current rating)
Step Two: RL/GL = CL (Current rating versus lefties)
Step Three: $[(C \times .80 + CL \times .20) \times ([GL+GR]/100)] + [([100-GL-GR]/100) \times L]$ = lefty rating, updated.

The same formula applies to righties (Step Two is RR/GR = CR, substitute CR for CL, and R for L in Step Three).

The Yankees' updated rating versus righties is 4.84; versus lefties, it is 5.03.

Example 7. Updating bullpen ratings.   Our team-statistics sheet contains two facts about the bullpen, the innings pitched and earned runs allowed by relief pitchers. To get a new season bullpen rating, first we get the bullpen's ERA. Let's use the following team stats for one example:

TEAM	PRIOR YEAR RATING	GAME PLAYED	BULLPEN INNINGS	EARNED RUNS
CUBS	3.17	40	110	39
YANKS	2.66	42	124	38

The Cubs' bullpen ERA is computed by multiplying runs (39) by 9, giving 351, then dividing by innings (110), giving 3.19. Remember, each game played counts .01 percent. The Cubs have played 40 games, so we multiply 3.19 by .40, giving 1.276. Last year's share counts 60 percent (100−40 = 60), so we multiply last year's rating (3.17) by .60, giving 1.902. 1.276 + 1.902 gives 3.18, the rating for this year.

Let:

P = prior year ERA (3.17 for Cubs)
I = innings pitched by relievers this year (110 for Cubs)
E = earned runs against relievers this year (39 for Cubs)
G = games played this year (40 for Cubs)

Our formula is:

$$E \left[\frac{9}{I} \times \frac{G}{100} \right] + P \times \frac{100 - G}{100} = \text{new rating}$$

The Yankees' new rating is 2.70.

Example 8. Updating unearned run percent. Let's suppose the following information appears on our team stat sheets:

TEAM	EARNED RUNS ALLOWED	UNEARNED RUNS ALLOWED	GAMES	LAST YEAR'S UNEARNED RUN PERCENT
RED SOX	141	13	41	.108
PHILLIES	128	23	37	.101

First, we divide unearned runs (13 for the Red Sox) by earned runs (141), giving .092. Since one game is worth 1 percent, and the Red Sox have played 41 games, we multiply .092 by .41, giving .0377. If this year is worth .41, last year is worth .59, so we multiply last year's unearned run percent (.108) by .59, giving .0637. .0377 plus .0637 is .101, the updated unearned run percent for the Red Sox.

Let:

U = unearned runs (13 for Red Sox)
E = earned runs (141 for Red Sox)
G = games (41 for Red Sox)
L = last year's unearned run percent (.108 for Red Sox)

Then our formula is:

$$[U/E \times (G/100)] + [L \times ([100-G]/100)]$$
$$= \text{updated unearned run percent.}$$

The updated unearned run percent for the Phillies is .130.

Example 9. Computing predicted runs for each team, after the season starts.

The first thing we must do is compute a new defensive rating for the starting pitcher. Let's assume we have the following information on Tom Seaver and the Cincinnati Reds:

Reds' old bullpen rating: 4.21
Reds' updated bullpen rating: 3.02
Reds' old unearned run percent: .079
Reds' updated unearned run percent: .102

Seaver's last three starts were as follows:

INNINGS	EARNED RUNS	RATING BEFORE	RATING AFTER
9	0	.788	.758
9	1	.758	.738
6 1/3	3	.738	.753

The first step is to "double" the effect of his last three starts. To do this, you see how much his rating changed in his last three starts. Seaver's rating was .788 before his last three starts, and .753 after, so it went down .035. To double the effect, we subtract .035 from his current rating, .753, getting .718. Next, we want to adjust .718 to account for the change in the Reds' bullpen performance. To do this, get the difference between the old and updated bullpen rating (4.21 − 3.02 = 1.19) and divide by 22 (the average percentage of any given game that the bullpen will pitch), giving .054. Since the Reds' bullpen has improved, we want to lower Seaver's rating, so we subtract .054 from .718, giving .664. Now we must adjust for the Reds' unearned run percent. To do this, get the difference between the old and updated unearned run percent (.102 − .079 = .023). Since the Reds are worse in fielding, we add .023 to Seaver's rating of .664, giving .687, the rating we will use to calculate the predicted runs for his opponents. Let's say he is pitching against the Dodgers, whose updated offensive rating against right-handers is 4.98. We multiply 4.98 by .687, giving 3.42, the predicted number of runs the Dodgers will score against Seaver.

Let:

$$O = \text{pitcher's rating before last three starts}$$
$$C = \text{current rating}$$
$$OB = \text{old bullpen rating}$$
$$B = \text{new bullpen rating}$$
$$OU = \text{old unearned percent}$$

U = new unearned percent
R = opponent's offensive rating

Then our formula is:

$$[C + C - O + \frac{OB - B}{22} - (OU - U)] \times R = \text{predicted runs}$$

Here are the facts on Tommy John and the Dodgers. We will assume he is facing the Reds, who have an updated rating of 4.95 against lefties.

Dodgers' old bullpen rating: 3.68
Dodgers' updated bullpen rating: 3.81
Dodgers' old unearned run percent: .103
Dodgers' updated unearned run percent: .101
Tommy John's rating before his last three starts was .794.
His current rating is .869.
The predicted number of runs he will allow the Reds is 4.69.

5 | Betting Baseball —The Total Experience

As I sit here now, writing this book, it is the middle of May, 1978. So far, I am ahead twenty-eight units on this baseball season (meaning I am ahead twenty-eight times the amount I bet on each game). I wonder about giving away my secrets for the price of this book. Since I bet into the opening line for the most part, if you start betting my teams, it probably won't hurt my odds, but I wonder. Well, it's too late to turn back now.

Although I am now well on my way to my fifth straight winning season, betting baseball is not all sunshine. I know of no other betting opportunity where the issue stays in doubt so long, or the unexpected happens so often. I remember once having a bet on Kansas City against Texas. It was the bottom of the ninth, and KC was up 4–1. Texas had two outs and a man on first, and the batter hit a pop-up behind first. Cookie Rojas was the Royals' second baseman, and the announcer said he was under it, and the game was over. That turned out to be a false assumption, since Rojas dropped the pop-up, and Texas went on to win the game. Rojas was probably one of the most fundamentally sound players in all of baseball. I wouldn't be surprised if it was the only pop-up he ever dropped in his life. But he dropped that one, and it cost me two thousand bucks. Or yesterday, I had the Yankees over the Royals, and a two-run lead with two out, two on in the ninth. Amos Otis hit a lazy fly to right center, Paul Blair trotted over and caught it, and Reggie Jackson plowed into him and knocked the ball loose. Otis merrily circled the bases while Blair glared at Jackson and my money went down the tube.

Probably the most frustrating, painful day in my gambling career came in 1975. It was in July, and I was up over forty thousand for the season, and betting two thousand a game. That particular night, a Friday, I went to the movies at around 9:00 P.M. At the time, I was tied or ahead in every game. When I got out of the movies I had lost every game but one, and that was Catfish Hunter versus the Twins. The game had been delayed by rain, and the Yankees were up 4–0 going into the ninth. Since Hunter was a 2–1 favorite, the game meant six thousand dollars to me. My other disasters had already cost me seventeen thousand for the night. Until that day, seven thousand had been the biggest single loss of my life. Needless to say, I was in a state of shock. Especially when the Twins bombed Hunter for four runs in the bottom of the ninth.

When I got home, I tuned the game in, and the Yankees had the bases loaded. They didn't score. The Twins went down one, two, three, and I breathed again. The next inning, Roy White led off with a triple. They didn't score. The Twins went down one, two, three. They kept it up until the fifteenth inning. The Yankees came within inches of scoring every inning. Balls caught up against the fence, runners thrown out at the plate, et cetera. Meanwhile, the Twins went down inning after inning, like pussycats. As they started the fifteenth, the announcer said this would be the last inning, due to the American League curfew. If the Yankees didn't score, the best I could do was tie. Remember, bets on suspended games do not carry over to their completion, so it was now or never for the Yankees. They went down one, two, three. I was staring a $21,000 loss right in the eye. I couldn't stand it. I turned off the radio. I waited for what seemed like hours—but must have only been a few minutes —and turned it on again. Bases loaded, no outs. I turned it off. I counted to 100, and turned it on. Three balls, no strikes. I listened, dazed, as the batter took three straight strikes. Two outs. I turned it off and counted to 100 again. My heart was pounding when I switched it back on. ". . . and the game will be completed prior to tomorrow's regularly scheduled game." Super. I had lost only $17,000. (The Yankees got five runs in the sixteenth inning the next day, and won 9–5. The dirty rats.) To this day, I have never equaled that feat— $17,000, and it was almost $21,000. Like I say, baseball is not all sunshine.

Maybe that's why I can give away my secrets so cheaply. Anyone who is willing to do all the work necessary, and has the stomach for the ups and downs of baseball betting, should come out on top.

Since I've told you about my worst betting experience, I should also tell you about my best. The best has nothing to do with a particular bet, or day of betting. The best is about money. In 1975, I had a safe deposit box in which I kept my winnings. As the season wore on, I put money in and took it out repeatedly, but I never counted it. I don't know why, just superstition, I guess. I had grown up poor, and had never been a saver, so I had never really had my hands on much cash. Money was a little intimidating to me. In 1974, I had wound up with a pretty good profit, but I had spent a lot of it by the end of the year. In 1975, I didn't spend a penny of my gambling earnings. It was all in the box. After the World Series, I made my last collection, and went to the bank to add it to my pile. I decided to count it. I had kept monthly figures on how I was doing, but I had not added them up, so, although I had a rough idea how much was there, I didn't really know how much.

The money was in envelopes, so first I emptied each envelope. Wow, I had a big pile of money. I just felt it for a while, just sort of weighing it. I was aware that I had a silly grin on my face, but there was no one around to see it. I sorted the money into denominations. It was almost all one-hundred-dollar bills. Then I started making stacks of one thousand, still not totaling it up. Finally, I started counting the stacks. My smile got bigger when I hit twenty thousand and was not even half done! Thirty thousand and still lots of nice, neat stacks to count. Forty thousand, and not as many stacks. Fifty thousand. Almost done. Fifty-six thousand, four hundred. I had won $56,400. I got goose bumps. It was the thrill of my betting career, counting that money. It was better than being in love.

For those of you who are prepared for the vagaries of baseball betting, but don't want to spend the time required to use my system, there are other approaches. They don't present as many betting opportunities, and the profits aren't as spectacular, but they don't require nearly as much work, and they can be used on the games to which the system doesn't apply.

The best non-system technique is the "ten worst pitchers in baseball" approach. This technique is deadly for the first month of the season. After that, the profits drop, as the betting opportunities get fewer and farther between.

The theory behind this technique is this: the bookie line is too team oriented. They adjust it for pitchers, but not enough when a pitcher is much worse than the average for his team. For example, the 1978 Cincinnati Reds had three pretty good pitchers in Tom Seaver, Fred Norman, and Bill Bonham. Their fourth starter was Tom Hume, not even close in ability to the Reds' other starters. If all the Reds' starters were as bad as Hume, they wouldn't even come close to being a .500 team. This was evident in 1977, when their starters other than Seaver and Norman were under .500. Yet, Hume was consistently a favorite, and frequently a big favorite the first month of the 1978 season, and he lost consistently. Since the Reds' overall record was good, Hume continued to be the favorite almost every time out, and he continued to lose. The linemakers were afraid to make the Reds the underdog to an inferior team. But with Hume pitching, the Reds *were* the inferior team. The linemakers never compensate enough when a rotation pitcher is much worse than the rest of a team's rotation pitchers.

So this technique involves determining which ten pitchers that are rotation starters are the most below average for their teams. The first step is to determine what each team's starting rotation will be. To do this, you just check the box scores every day for the first few days of the season. Some teams use a five-man rotation, but most start out with a four-man rotation. When you have determined every team's rotation, you just get the average earned-run average for a team's rotation. (For a four-man rotation, you add the four starters' ERAs and divide by four. For a five-man rotation, you add the five starters' ERAs and divide by five. The Cincinnati Reds started the 1978 season with a four-man rotation of Tom Seaver, Bill Bonham, Fred Norman, and Tom Hume. Hume was much the worst pitcher in this rotation. The Dodgers started the season with a rotation of Burt Hooton, Tommy John, Don Sutton, Rick Rhoden and Doug Rau. There was not a great deal of difference between these five based on their 1977 performances.) Next subtract the average from the worst ERA of the starters. When you have done this for all twenty-six teams, take the ten pitchers with the biggest difference, and they are your "ten worst pitchers." Bet against them every time they pitch until the season is one month old. Most years this will get you a profit of at least ten units. In 1978, it was worth 25.8 units; 1977 wasn't as good, because five of the worst ten were out of the rotation within two weeks, so it only won 11.2 units. But that first month is like money in the bank.

After the first month, you only keep betting against your "ten worst pitchers" if they still have the worst ERA among the team's starters. Usually, three or four of them will survive until the middle of June before they either shape up or ship out. I keep betting against them until they are no longer the worst pitchers on the team.

For those of you using the system described in the earlier chapters, the system will almost always bet against these pitchers, but when it doesn't, bet against them anyway. They are terrific to bet against. I just wish they would stick around longer and pitch more often.

Another non-system technique I use involves rookie pitchers. Rookies are more emotional about their jobs than veterans. If they do well, they get all psyched up, and feel unbeatable. If they do poorly, they get worried about getting sent back to the minors, and they press too hard. As a result, rookies are very prone to streaks, much more so than the blasé veteran pitchers. The idea behind my rookie betting technique is to get on a rookie's bandwagon when he is hot, and bet against him when he gets cold.

I consider a pitcher a rookie if he is twenty-five years old or younger, and has never pitched more than fifty innings in a previous season, *or* has just come up from the minors during the season. I put a rookie on my "bet-on" list if he has a start that meets the following qualifications:

1. He pitches at least seven innings.
2. He allows two or fewer runs.
3. He allows fewer hits than innings pitched.

Once a rookie gets on the list, I bet on him every time he pitches, until he gets knocked out before pitching five innings in which he gives up more runs than innings pitched.

Over the past few seasons, some of the "hot" rookies have been spectacular winners, like Mark Fidrych, Ron Guidry, and Dave Rozema.

I put a rookie on my "bet-against" list when he meets the following qualifications:

1. More hits per inning in last start, or walks plus hits are double the innings pitched.
2. At least as many runs allowed as innings pitched.
3. He was not on the "bet-on" list for his last start.

Once a rookie gets on the "bet-against" list, I bet against him every time, until he pitches a game that gets him on the "bet-on" list, or pitches a complete game victory.

The "bad" rookies tend not to last very long, but you can cash quite a few bets before they get shipped out to the minors.

One last "non-system" technique involves injuries. The effect of key injuries is definitely underrated by the line-makers and betting public. It takes at least a week before the line adjusts for an injury to a key player. To me, a key player is the third or fourth hitter in a team's batting order. Most third and fourth hitters are worth around twenty cents on the line. But I don't think the linemakers make any adjust-ments initially. So when I know a key player is not going to play, and it is a game I have not made a system line on, I bet against the team with the key injury for one week if the opposing pitcher pitches with the arm opposite to the in-jured player's batting side. In other words, if the injured player bats right-handed, I will bet against his team if they are facing a left-handed pitcher.

If you are not using the system, you can bet every game that meets the above criteria. Over the past few seasons, injuries to players like George Brett, Reggie Jackson, Mike Schmidt, Joe Morgan, and Richie Zisk have led me to some nice profits. As good as these players are, the linemakers don't adjust adequately to the difference they make to a team.

Until now, I have described "rules" for betting baseball. Ninety percent of my bets on baseball are based on rules for betting. The other 10 percent are intuitive bets based on "handicapping" the games. Most gamblers are hand-icappers, or intuitive bettors. In other words, they do not use formulas and rules for betting, but weigh all the infor-mation on a game and decide who to bet based on their judgment. This requires a degree of objectivity and men-tal health that very few gamblers possess. I do not recom-mend intuitive betting on baseball, but if that's how you want to do it, here are a few pointers on "handicapping" baseball.

First, you must have as much information as you can get

to be a baseball handicapper. That means reading every box score, the weekly batting and pitching averages, all the newspaper articles, listening to as many games as you can, and watching as many games as you can.

Second, you should concentrate on the teams you can get the most information on, the local teams, the teams you can watch, listen to, and read about. I concentrate on the Cubs and White Sox when I'm living in Chicago, the Dodgers and the Angels when I'm in Las Vegas. If you are betting intuitively, only bet games involving the teams you know well. It is impossible to keep track of twenty-six teams in your head. At best, you will have a general impression of what most teams are like. There are about eighty games played every week in the major leagues. Unless you keep records—in which case you should use my system—you will not remember everything you need to be an expert on every team. So, stick to the teams you know everything about.

The first thing I want to know about a team is the tendencies of the manager. Most baseball experts say the manager is worth seven or eight games a year. I think the best manager is worth twenty to thirty games a year compared to the worst manager. Frequently, managers will change their approach during the course of a season. When they change for the better, the team will improve. When they change for the worse, the team will lose more.

Here are the things I look for from managers:

1.   How stable is his batting order?
The most important job a manager has is to decide on fielding assignments and batting order. If he is constantly changing lineups and batting orders, then he either doesn't trust his own judgment, or he doesn't trust his players' abilities. Platooning and lineup juggling are signs of weakness. A set lineup is good. A constantly changing lineup is bad.

2. Does he use an intelligent batting order?

This can make an enormous difference in the number of runs a team scores. Each spot in the batting order calls for a specific type of hitter, and putting the wrong kind of hitter in the wrong spot can really hurt a team. This is an area where managers do a lot of adjusting during a season, and the right adjustments can really help, whereas the wrong adjustments can ruin a team. In 1977, Billy Hunter worked miracles with the Texas Rangers when he took over, just because he changed to a better batting order and a set lineup. Here are my guidelines for what a batting order should look like. I use the 1978 Cincinnati Reds or Boston Red Sox as my examples of a perfect lineup.

Leadoff—the hitter with the best reached-base percentage who is also a singles hitter. Reasoning: He will come up with fewer men on base than anyone on the team, so power would be wasted in this spot. But he will lead off more innings than anyone else, so he should be good at getting on base. For the Reds, Pete Rose is the ideal leadoff hitter. Note that Rose is not nearly as fast as several other Reds. Putting an extremely fast man first is a mistake that is commonly made by managers. The first-place hitter does not come up with a double-play situation very much, and you want your speed coming up with a man on first and less than two outs. Rick Burleson of Boston is a very similar hitter.

Second hitter—a super speedball who is a leg hitter, and can hit behind the runner. Reasoning: If your second hitter gets to first rapidly, he is going to be on first base with second unoccupied more than any hitter on the team. This is where the most stolen-base opportunities will come. The second hitter will often come up with a man on first and no outs, which means he will have the hole between first and second to hit through. If he succeeds, you will have runners on first and third. If he grounds into a force play, he will be on first. Because of the possibility of the second hitter reaching base on a force-out, he will be on first base more than any other hitter, especially the leadoff man. Wasting speed in the leadoff spot is crazy. The Reds use Ken Griffey, the fastest man on the team, as their second-place hitter. The Red Sox use Jerry Remy, also their fastest man. Both are left-handed.

Third-place hitter—this should be the best all-around hitter on the team. He should hit for power and average, and he should have enough speed to avoid double plays. Reasoning: The third hitter is going to come up with base runners and less than two outs more than anyone on the team. He has to have enough power to get the RBIs, but he'll need speed to avoid the double play. He is also batting in front of the most powerful hitters on the team, so he should be able to reach base often so he can be driven in. On the Reds, Joe Morgan fits the bill perfectly. (Note: Morgan was having injury problems in 1978, which hurt the Reds. In his earlier years he was the perfect third hitter.) Jim Rice is clearly the Red Sox' best hitter.

Fourth-place hitter—the "clean-up" hitter, because he gets to "clean" the bases. The team's best power hitter should bat fourth. Reasoning: Obviously, the fourth hitter is going to get the most RBI chances. On the Reds, George Foster is perfect. Carl Yastrzemski is Mr. Cleanup for Boston.

Fifth-place hitter—The slowest power hitter on the team. Reasoning: The fifth hitter comes up with two outs more than any other hitter on the team. This means fewer opportunities to hit into double plays, so speed isn't essential. Also, a high "reached-base percentage" is not important with two outs. But he must have power to protect the clean-up hitter. The other team must fear the fifth hitter or the clean-up hitter will never get a good pitch to hit in the clutch. The Reds use Johnny Bench; slow, but an excellent power hitter who hits for a low average. The perfect fifth hitter. Carlton Fisk is Boston's powerful slow poke.

Sixth-place hitter—decent power, decent speed, decent reached-base percentage. Reasoning: The sixth-place hitter will lead off more innings than anyone except the leadoff man, so he needs to reach base often. But he has worse hitters behind him, so he needs more speed to get around the bases easier. He will also come up in more RBI situations than the leadoff man, so he needs more power than the leadoff man. The Reds use Dan Driessen, who fits this description exactly. I think you can tell more about a team's offense by looking at the sixth hitter than anything else. Look at the top teams in 1978. Driessen on the Reds, Baker on the Dodgers, Lynn on the Red Sox, Chambliss on the Yankees, Lezcano on the Brewers, Maddox on the Phillies. They all fit the profile— around twenty homers a year, good speed, .280-plus batting averages.

Seventh-place hitter—duplicate of the second hitter, only a little more power and less speed. Reasoning: He will be coming up in the same situations as the second-place hitter for the most part, except he will have worse hitters behind him, so his reaching base isn't as important, but his power is more important. On the Reds, Dave Concepcion; the second fastest man on the team, but not as good an average hitter as Griffey. The Red Sox don't have an ideal seventh hitter, because George Scott is too slow. But he is the logical choice considering their personnel. Eighth-place hitter—whatever is left—the worst hitter on the team in the National League. In the American League, the better hitter between the two that are left. The Reds use Geronimo in the eighth spot, clearly the worst hitter on the team. Boston uses Dwight Evans eighth, with Butch Hobson ninth. Personally, I would reverse them.

When Larry Doby took over the White Sox in 1978, he put Ralph Garr in the fifth spot in the White Sox lineup. Garr is a speedster with no power who hits for a good average. This was so wrong I couldn't believe Doby would do it. It convinced me he would be a flop, at least until he learned to manage. I made a lot of money betting against the White Sox after Doby took over.

If you see a manager settle on a lineup that fits the above description, you can expect good things. If he uses a lineup that doesn't make sense, it will hurt the team.

The next most important thing a manager has to do is decide when to change pitchers. I admire Sparky Anderson (Captain Hook) because he is very quick to change pitchers. The Reds' front office admired him less—they fired him. I believe they will regret this gross blunder. The 1978 Oakland As are a great argument for the quick hook. They stayed in contention most of the year with a collection of castoffs just by keeping a fresh pitcher in the game as much as any team I've ever seen. If you see a manager lose confidence in his bullpen, and start staying with his pitchers too long, watch out. It is a sure road to losing.

The actual strategy during a game decides very few games. But there are three things to look for that are signs of a bad manager. First, does he have non-pitchers sacrifice-bunt? If he does, he is an idiot. The idea is *not* to make an out. To make outs on purpose is crazy. They will argue that they are playing for one run. This only makes sense if that one run wins the game right then and there. The big inning wins games. (It is a well-known sucker bet that the winning team will score more runs in its biggest scoring inning than the losing team scores the whole game). The intentional walk is another piece of bad strategy, especially early in the game. Again, the idea is to get the other side out, not put them on base on purpose. The intentional walk that loads the bases is particularly dumb, because of the pressure it puts on the pitcher. The third piece of strategy that separates the good and bad managers is the use of the "take" sign. The take sign is used to tell the hitter he is not permitted to swing at a pitch. On 2-0, 3-0, and 3-1 counts it is the manager's job to decide whether or not the hitter should be allowed to swing. The hitters want to swing because they think they will get a fat pitch to hit. If a manager is afraid of his players or wants to be Mr. Nice Guy, he will rarely give the take sign on 2-0 and 3-1 counts. So, if you see a team consistently swinging at 2-0 and 3-1 pitches, particularly when they are losing and no one is on base, then you are looking at a weak manager.

If you watch a team regularly, you will soon understand the

manager's basic approach to his job. It is most important to notice changes for the better or worse. I have seen many teams turn around because of changes in strategy, or changes in managers. In 1977, the White Sox switched from Paul Richards to Bob Lemon, and they made several other personnel changes. Richards was a "defensive" manager. I swear he even wanted his designated hitter to be a good fielder. He managed as if every game was going to be 1–0, lots of sacrifices, intentional walks, hit and runs, et cetera. As a result, the White Sox didn't score much. Lemon, on the other hand, played for the big inning, rarely sacrificing. The result? The White Sox became a run-scoring machine in 1977. (Bert Campaneris of the Rangers had more sacrifice bunts in 1977 than the entire White Sox team).

When the manager starts violating the percentages I've outlined above, the team is worth betting against until the line starts to reflect the results. When he manages sensibly, the team is worth betting on until the linemakers catch on. So you must know how he is managing if you are going to be a baseball handicapper.

The second thing I want to know about a team is, are they fastball hitters, breaking-ball hitters, low-ball hitters, or high-ball hitters? You can only get this information by watching the games. Most pitchers fall into one of two categories. Either they are power pitchers, who rely on throwing the ball so hard the hitters can't react in time, or they rely on finesse, throwing for spots, and movement and location. Of course, the truly superior pitchers, like Palmer and Seaver, have both power and finesse. In watching a pitcher to determine which category he falls into, the key is his fastball. Power pitchers throw a rising fastball, finesse pitchers throw a sinking fastball. Power pitchers throw at least 80 percent fastballs, finesse pitchers only about 50 percent fastballs. Watch your teams and see how they do when facing both types of pitchers when the pitcher is "on." A pitcher is on when he is throwing the ball where he wants to. Most hitters will do very well when the pitcher is not getting the ball where he wants it. To tell if the pitcher is getting the ball where he wants it, watch the catcher. He will hold his glove where he wants the pitcher to throw the ball. When a pitcher is on, he will consistently (75 percent of the time) get the ball within six inches of the catcher's target.

Try to watch every game and decide the following:

1. Is the pitcher a power, finesse, or combination pitcher?
2. Is he hitting his target?
3. Is he being hit hard?

Soon you will have a good idea of the team's tendencies. Are they fastball hitters, high-ball hitters? If you decide they are fastball hitters, then you know they are a pretty good bet against a power pitcher. If you decide they hit sinker pitchers well, they are a good bet against a sinker-baller.

In 1977, the White Sox were murder against power pitchers, or any pitcher who relied on his fastball to get hitters out. In contrast, sinker pitchers gave them fits. So I bet on them whenever they faced a flamethrower, like Nolan Ryan, and against them when they faced a sinker-baller, like Arroyo of the Tigers. (Of course, these weren't the only factors, but they were major factors in my betting decisions.)

This year (1978) the Cubs are a breaking-ball hitting team. They have four or five guys who can't get around on a good fastball, so I tend to bet against them when they see Candelaria, Vida Blue, or Craig Swan, and bet on them against Ross Grimsley or Jerry Koosman.

As a general rule, power pitchers have trouble with power hitters, and finesse pitchers have a hard time with singles hitters. I watch how each pitcher pitches every type of hitter, and how they do against him when he is on, or hitting the target. For example, Steve Stone of the White Sox is murder pitching against right-handed power hitters. So he is a good bet against Boston or Texas, teams that are overloaded with right-handed power hitters. He does his worst against left-handed hitters that are not pull hitters, and weak right-handed hitters. The Yankees kill him with Mickey Rivers, Chambliss, and Jackson.

If you concentrate on the kind of hitters that give each pitcher trouble, soon you will have a good feel for which teams they can beat, and which teams will beat them.

Finally, I look for the "key" player in each team's offense. When the key player is hot, the team is usually hot. When he is cold, the team is usually cold. In 1977, Ralph Garr was the key man on the White Sox. In 1978, Dave Kingman was the key man on the Cubs. If a team doesn't have a key man, it is much more difficult to anticipate how well they will do. In 1978, the White Sox didn't have a spark plug, and I didn't do nearly as well betting their games as I usually do. But I made up for it with the Cubs, because I knew Kingman's pattern, and it made the difference.

So, for me, handicapping a baseball game is weighing the factors, then deciding if there is a good betting opportunity in view of the line on the game. Basically, I check the following items:

1. Has the manager changed for the better or worse?
2. Is the opposing pitcher the type the Chicago team usually hits?
3. Is the opposing team the type that usually hits the Chicago pitcher?
4. Is the key player hot or cold?
5. Which pitcher do I think is better?
6. Which team do I think is better?

If a lot of pluses stack up for either side, and the line on the game is attractive, I bet. If not, I pass. It isn't really scientific, so I can't give you a formula, or promise you the same results I get. But if you think about the things I've listed, and if you have the knack for it, you can win at handicapping. Not too many people can, which is why I recommend the system, or the non-system techniques, or both.

There are several reasons why I don't recommend intuitive betting on baseball. First, if you are a baseball fan, you probably have a favorite team. For almost everyone, myself included, this means your judgment will be clouded by your emotional preference. There is no way to make money on "heart" bets unless you are just plain lucky. I have nothing against luck, but I know you can't count on it. It has taken me years to get myself to bet against the White Sox, except with system bets. I have finally reached a point where winning is important enough to me to make betting against them possible, and I still couldn't swear to you that some of my bets aren't emotional. I win betting Sox games, but I win more betting Cub games, so the emotional factor is probably still present. If you are not a fan, this factor won't interfere. If you are, you are flirting with disaster when you bet games involving your favorite team.

Another problem with many handicappers is the tendency to want to bet the team they think will win, regardless of the line. It is very difficult to "intuit" what the line "should" be. So a lot of bettors find themselves constantly betting the favorite, regardless of how high the line is. In fact, I have one friend, Art, who bets *only* favorites. Once, he called me up and asked me what I thought of the Yankees against the Orioles. I told him I liked the Yankees. He said he liked them too, and asked me what the line was. I told him the line was 1.40. He said great, get him the Yankees for two hundred bucks. I said, "Okay, you have the Yankees plus 1.30 for two hundred." "Plus 1.30? The Yankees are the dogs?" he asked. When I told him yes, he said he didn't want them if they were the underdogs. He thought they were the favorite, and were supposed to win. He didn't want them if they were supposed to lose.

Although he is the extreme favorite player, his thinking is the kind of thing that gets handicappers in trouble. They are more interested in winning the bet than in having the edge. If you are going to handicap, I recommend only betting underdogs that you think should be favorites, or small favorites that you think should be big favorites.

Another drawback to handicapping is the danger of being overly influenced by one event. You may see a game on television in which a pitcher looks unbeatable. The next time out, it will be very hard not to bet on him, even if the line seems like the right line. That may have been his only good start of the year, but in your mind you can see him mowing them down forever. So you bet on him. Even if he loses, if you don't watch him pitch, your mental image of him will still be of when he pitched like a champion. So you bet him again and again, until you have wiped out that picture in your head. It happens to bettors every day. They base their bets on too little evidence. If you handicap, it is very difficult to keep all your facts equal. You will prefer some facts over others, and this defeats most people.

If, in spite of all my arguments, you still prefer to bet intuitively, good luck. But I know you would be better off betting scientifically.

You should now have enough information to decide whether or not baseball betting is for you, and which technique suits you best. If you do want to bet baseball, I hope you live in Nevada, which is the only place where it is legal. I have moved to Nevada myself for that very reason. It is probably illegal for me to give you advice on how to locate a bookmaker, so I will leave that problem to you. If you just happen to find one, he has my sympathy.

6 | Pro-Football Betting—The Components

The National Football League, or National Football Lottery, as Larry Merchant so aptly describes it, is the most bet-on sport in this country. What with parlay cards, office pools, friendly bets between fans, and, of course, the ever-obliging bookies, everyone bets football. The point spread on the local favorites is a more widely known fact than the Dow Jones average. Teenagers bet football, secretaries bet football, grandmothers bet football. I even knew a minister who bet football. Betting is the backbone of the sport. Kill the point spread, and pro football would go back to being second-rate. Jimmy the Greek has done as much for pro football as O.J. Simpson.

I love it. I've been betting football since I was fourteen. I used to bet college football too, but now I am a purist. Only the best man-mountains are worthy of my attention. Boy, oh boy, those guys have gotten big. I met a lineman once in Las Vegas, and it isn't the shoulder pads that make them look so huge. My nickname is "Giant," but next to him I was "Dwarf." I didn't have the nerve to ask him what he thought of the point spread on his next game. If he had been offended, he might have sacked me, and I have never been fond of broken bones.

Since it would be un-American not to consider betting football, let us look at this great sport as a betting opportunity.

1.   What are the betting rules?

There are several ways to bet football. The way I prefer is the straight bet against the point spread. One team is favored to win by a certain number of points. You may either give the points and bet the favorite, or take the points and bet the underdog. The favorite wins if they win the game by more points than the point spread, the underdog wins if they don't lose the game by the point spread, and it is a tie if the favorite wins by exactly the point spread.

There are "teasers," which allow you to alter the point spread, but get worse odds. For example, with a 12-point, three-team teaser, you must lay 6–5, and select three teams who do not lose to the point spread by 12 points.

There are parlays, where you select more than one team, all of which must win. (Ties do not lose, and the bet reverts to the price for a parlay with one less team).

There are parlay cards, where you must pick all winners (from three to ten games) and ties lose.

There are over and unders, where you bet that the total number of points in a game will be over or under a specified number.

And, lately, some bookies are putting out odds on the games, with no point spread.

2.   What is the bookie's take, or house percentage?

This depends on the kind of bet you make. If you bet a single game with the point spread, you must lay 11–10, which means a 4.7-percent take for the bookie. On a two-team parlay, you get 13–5, which is a 10-percent edge for the bookie. On a three-team parlay, you get 6–1, which is a 12.5-percent edge for the bookie. It gets worse and worse as you add teams. (At 11–10, you are betting eleven dollars. If there was no bookie take, you should get back twenty-two dollars if you win. But you don't, you only get back twenty-one dollars. So the bookie keeps one dollar out of every 22, or 4.7 percent. On a two-team parlay, the odds should be 15–5, not 13–5. So the bookie is paying you eighteen dollars instead of twenty. That's two bucks out of twenty, or 10 percent.)

Teasers are harder to figure, because the value of the extra points is not that easy to figure. I looked at teasers for two seasons, and the take varied from 8 percent to 13 percent on the ones I studied. Enough to keep me from playing them.

Parlay cards take a minimum of 25 percent, so they aren't even worth thinking about. The money line varies a lot, but it is always worse than 4.7 percent.

Stick to straight bets and 4.7 percent. Since you get to do the choosing, the percentage isn't too big to be beatable.

3. Who is the competition? (Who are you really betting against?)

Football is very similar to baseball in that you are betting against the linemaker, whose line is altered somewhat by the bettors. Football bettors include more fans than baseball, and, therefore, a smaller percentage of professionals. There is more emotional betting on football than on baseball, and a higher percentage of the games are on television, which leads to a lot of betting for entertainment. So, all in all, I would say the competition is a little weaker than in baseball. I view the competition as a negative factor in football. I wish the linemakers weren't involved. I would prefer a pari-mutuel pool.

4. Is the game honest?

I don't think there is any way to fix a game involving so many individual players. There was one fix scandal a long time ago, and Hornung and Karras got caught betting on themselves, but there is no evidence of any fixing. The number of players you run into in Las Vegas is a little disturbing, because Las Vegas is full of gamblers, and I would rather not have the players talking to gamblers, but a single player would have a hard time fixing a game. As far as I'm concerned, football is an honest game.

5. What information is available to you?

This is pro football's biggest drawback for the systematic gambler. For the most part, the available statistics are strictly team statistics. The individual statistics relate primarily to quarterbacks, running backs, and receivers. Linemen are statistical nonentities for the fans, and they determine the outcome of most games. This makes it impossible to evaluate the effect of injuries, compare each lineman to his adversary, et cetera.

What you do get is points scored, first downs, running yardage, passing yardage, turnovers, penalty yards, kicking and receiving information. It isn't much, but it is better than nothing.

You can watch around 25 percent of the games, which does help a lot. You can also listen to tons of analysis on TV and the radio, and read tons of analysis in the newspapers. Most of it is garbage, unfortunately. Keep track of the TV commentators' and sports writers' predictions sometime. If they are betting on their predictions, they better get awfully big salaries. Gerald Strine is an exception. He knows his stuff.

There are several good books on football. My favorite is by Gerald Strine and Neil Isaacs, *Covering the Spread: How to Bet Pro Football. Gambling Times* magazine, as well as *Sports Form,* frequently publish informative articles. *The Gold Sheet* and *Pro Football News* also have a lot to offer. But the lack of comprehensive statistical information is still a problem.

6. Is there information available to the competition that isn't available to you?

Unless you are in on the injury grapevine, you bet there is! My friend Herschel is plugged into the injury grapevine, so I have access to a lot of information that is not public knowledge. And not a week goes by when I don't get at least three key injuries before they are published (if they ever are). The line always reflects these "secret" injuries sooner or later, so the competition knows about them.

Also, the linemakers have access to local experts who see every game their team plays, know players well enough to get clued in on team morale, and can assess the overall physical condition of the team. A big plus for the linemaker, a big minus for us, and a major drawback to betting on the NFL.

7. Do you like the game?

Doesn't everyone? Larry Little leading the power sweep, knocking tiny Rod Perry into the grandstands; Pittsburgh's "Iron Curtain" of Joe Greene, Steve Furness, Dwight White, and L.C. Greenwood tearing opposing quarterbacks apart; Larry Csonka colliding head-on with Bill Bergey, as the stadium shakes; Walter Payton running into a mass of humanity and emerging unscathed; O.J. Simpson showing a would-be tackler his body, then darting away as the defender tackles air; Lynn Swann springing into the clear, then tantalizingly gliding into the path of the ball; Fred Biletnikoff sneaking away from defenders, then making an impossible catch; Dave Kasper lumbering downfield with tacklers hanging on him, getting a free ride; Rick Upchurch dodging and dancing, then bursting past the defense on his way to another long kick return; the suicide squads, the special teams, hurling their bodies at each other at top speed to prove they have the guts to play this "man's game." Professional football is violent, graceful, swift, tense, strategic, brutal, subtle, and unpredictable. It can also be methodical, one-sided, comical, inept, and boring, as are most Super Bowls.

It is the most frustrating, exhilarating and surprising sport to bet on. I have watched teams completely dominate a game and lose. It is not uncommon to lose to the point spread because each team puts winning the game ahead of winning your bet for you—this is the big disadvantage of betting point spreads. Football also produces the most sudden, dramatic, and unexpected turnarounds. I once had a bet on the Chiefs where I was giving 8 points. With thirty seconds to go, the opposition (whom I don't remember) scored a touchdown, cutting the Chiefs' lead to 4 points. There was no way I could win the game. The other team was a cinch to try an onside kick. If it worked, they would have the ball, and an interception runback was my only chance. If it didn't work, the Chiefs would run the clock out. So, they kicked the ball about ten yards, angling for the sideline. Bobby Bell caught it on the fly, on the dead run, and ran down the field untouched for a meaningless (to the Chiefs) touchdown, and I won my bet. I've never seen that happen before or since.

In the most frustrating game I ever lost (a Pittsburgh-Oakland game), during the last play of the game, the ball was batted away by Jack Tatum. Just as the Oakland players and I began to dance with joy, Franco Harris snatched the ball out of the air and raced down the sidelines for the most disgusting, lucky touchdown I've ever seen.

There's no doubt about it; I love football.

8. What special abilities do you bring to the situation?

The things that can help you beat the point spreads are a thorough understanding of the game, access to the injury grapevine, the ability to watch a game and remember a lot of details, a knack for numbers, a knowledge of statistics, knowledge of and access to computers, an understanding of group psychology, access to several lines on the games, and good instincts for "seeing" the strengths and weaknesses of a team while you watch a game.

I have all those qualities, except for the understanding of the psychology of football teams. Herschel, my friend from previous chapters, is fantastic at telling which teams will be "up" and which teams will be "down." I lose several bets a year bucking his intuition. This year, I swore I'd listen to his strong "hunches."

My understanding of football is not a super-strong point because I never played the game much. I have watched at least a thousand football games, and read reams of articles on the subject. But there are many people who know more about the intricacies of the game.

What I do have is a strange talent, apparently a rare one, which I call my own "instant replay." For a few hours after I have watched a game, I can recall every play in some detail. For a few minutes after a play, I can re-visualize it almost exactly, so anything that didn't register the first time is there for me to see on my own "instant replay." This gives me a very strong impression of the ability of all the players. Most people, myself included, concentrate on the ball, which gives you information about what is happening on center stage. But after the play I turn on my "instant replay" and take note of what else happened, away from the ball.

Of course, the computer always helps, and my willingness to spend hours punching buttons on a calculator helps. I can bet against lines in three different cities, so I can usually get a 1/2-point or point difference in the spread on a game, and sometimes as much as 2 points. Herschel keeps me tuned in on the injuries. So football is a sport in which my abilities fit very well, although not quite as well as in baseball.

To summarize the pluses and minuses of football betting: The biggest minus is lack of information; also, the prime source of competition, the linemakers, possesses an information edge.

The game is honest, has a reasonable house edge, and there is plenty of opportunity to watch games on TV. If you like the game and have some of the special abilities needed, it definitely offers an opportunity to win some money. The question is, what is the best approach to beating the point spread?

There are four basic football teams within each team: the offensive team, the defensive team, the special teams for kickoffs and punt returns, and the placekicking team. These teams truly function independently of each other, except that their effectiveness affects the situation for the other teams. They practice separately, have separate plays, for the most part different coaches, players, and captains. Within each of the teams, there are other divisions. The offense passes and runs, and every player must use different skills depending on which kind of play is being used. The quarterback plays a minor role on a running play, and is the major key to success on a pass. The blocking back must block one way on a pass, another on a run. The running back starts out in a crowd on a running play, and must catch a football and run in relatively open territory on a pass, the flankers block on runs, catch the ball and run with it on passes. The point is, a player's skills will probably differ for both kinds of plays, sometimes greatly. Gale Sayers was a tremendous runner, but he couldn't catch. Joe Namath's entire offensive line in his heyday with the Jets blocked superbly on passes, but poorly on runs. The running and passing games even break down into two parts each: the sweep versus the inside run, and the short pass versus the long pass. Again, the skills involved are different. The guard who is tough inside may lack the speed to lead a power sweep effectively; the flanker who has the quickness to get open on short passes may not have the speed for the long bomb.

This diversity of necessary talent is seen on defense, too. Dick Butkus may have been the greatest linebacker of all time against the run, but he was only fair against the pass unless he was blitzing the quarterback. The point is, football can be broken down into teams within teams, and then components within teams, as follows:

OFFENSE

RUN   PASS

SWEEP INSIDE   LONG SHORT

continued

continued

SPECIAL TEAMS

PUNTS   KICKOFFS

RETURN DEFENSE   RETURN DEFENSE

DEFENSE

RUN   PASS

SWEEP INSIDE   LONG SHORT

PLACEKICK TEAMS

KICKING   DEFENDING

There are seven components to a football game: the sweep, inside run, long pass, short pass, punt return, kickoff return, and placekick. Each of these components has an offensive and defensive side, so we have fourteen pairings to analyze—Team A's offensive capability in each of the seven components versus Team B's defensive capability in each of the seven components, and vice versa.

This is where the information gap is really painful. We can't get a statistical comparison on each of these subdivisions. The best we can get is run, pass, special teams, and some facts about placekicking, both offensively and defensively. Even these statistics have flaws, because they aren't broken down by quarter. When a score is one-sided, the statistics are distorted. So we are presented with limited—and somewhat misleading—statistics. The use of these statistics alone probably won't predict the outcome of the game well enough to produce a profit.

How do we improve the statistics? I came up with two separate approaches to the problem of betting football. The first involves a systematic, or objective approach to betting football. The second involves a subjective, or handicapper's approach to betting football. I use them both, though I prefer handicapping. Each involves comparing the offensive components against the corresponding defensive components.

Chapters 7 and 8 describe the handicapping approach. Chapter 9 outlines the systematic approach. The systematic approach involves a lot of calculations, so skip it if you hate figures. But my football system is a winning technique if you have the necessary patience.

7 | Handicapping the National Football League— the Team

Football is the only gambling opportunity in which I prefer handicapping to system betting. The lack of adequate statistical information is one reason, but the primary reason is that the first five weeks of the season produce so many good "common sense" bets. Anyway, my system doesn't apply until the sixth week of the season. My betting record for the first five weeks of each season over the past ten years is 201 wins, 101 losses, and 14 ties. In those ten years, I have made money every single year on the first five weeks. I improved that record by winning 21 and losing 8 the first five weeks of the 1978 season.

I also find the playoffs and the Super Bowl to represent exceptional betting opportunities, but for a different reason. The line on those games is pretty good, but the edge I have there is that the good teams get on television a lot. So I have had plenty of opportunity to see them firsthand, and thereby get a good picture of their strengths and weaknesses.

Handicapping football starts with understanding the philosophy of the organization behind each team. A successful team starts with a successful organization, from the owner down to the trainer. Some sports, like baseball, are games of individual brilliance. The championship Oakland As teams proved that. Other sports, like basketball, are team sports, where individuals must work together successfully to succeed. The Philadelphia 76ers of the 1977 and 1978 seasons proved that. But football is an organization sport. Individual brilliance is not the key ingredient, teamwork on the field is not the key ingredient: a coordinated organization is the key. Football is the only sport in which they practice more than they play. A team has six days to prepare for a single contest. The effectiveness of this preparation is incredibly important. It requires a smooth, coordinated, organized, and systematic approach on the part of scouts, coaches, players, and trainers. A weak scout can be just as harmful as a weak cornerback. A poor assistant coach will not prepare his team within the team effectively. The player who doesn't prepare mentally for the game is just as bad as the player who isn't physically prepared for the game. The trainer who isn't aware of all the physical problems on the team will not keep the coaches informed as to areas of potential weakness or breakdown.

Jerry Kramer's book, *Instant Replay*, will give you a sense of what I am talking about. The individual player has a job to do, but how he does it depends on the trainer, his individual coach, the team coach, scouting reports, and his own awareness of what he will be up against.

What does all this mean to us as handicappers? It is the cornerstone of most of my handicapping theories. The implications of the concept of football as an "organization" sport are far-reaching.

During my data-processing career, I gradually progressed through the managerial ranks from lead programmer to programming supervisor to manager of systems and programming, to director of data processing, to vice-president, where my responsibilities included the management of twelve departments and over two hundred people. At the lower levels of management, I adapted as much as possible to the individual's needs and talents. The higher I got, the more difficult this became. For a time, I became a poor manager, and I had a very difficult time accomplishing goals. It seemed that my managers and I were frequently working at cross purposes. Eventually, I realized the organization could not adapt to the individual once the organization had reached the point where a totally coordinated effort was required. I changed all my management theories. If the individual had to adapt to the organization, the organization had to have a basic philosophy that was clear to everyone. Individuals who could not adapt had to be replaced. A major factor in recruiting had to be the selection of individuals who fit the organization philosophy. My managers had to understand the basic philosophy, agree with it enough to follow it, and evaluate and manage their employees within the framework of the philosophy. They could adapt to their employees only within that framework.

The philosophy I adopted fit my preferences, and it was successful. It was just as important, if not more so, that I was able to work well within the framework of the philosophy. It doesn't really matter what the philosophy was; there are many different ways to run an organization successfully, so long as the entire organization is run consistently.

The successful football organizations have a consistent philosophy. They don't change their basic philosophy to suit a few individuals. This accounts for the predictability of the more successful teams. It accounts for the large number of individuals who improve dramatically when they change organizations. They may not fit into one team's approach, but they'll be perfect for another. This explains why so many stars, particularly the ones who play out their options, do poorly when they change teams. They don't fit their new team's philosophy. Successful teams draft players that will fit in. People are always amazed by the success of the Dallas first-round choices. But the answer is simple. Dallas has the best idea of what kind of player will fit in with their approach to the game—and many of their outstanding players would have been bums elsewhere. But the teams that draft the "best player available" don't get the job done if that player doesn't fit their philosophy.

My first rule for handicapping football is this: identify the successful organizations and know which teams have a winning record through several generations of players. (Four years is, to me, a generation of players.) Oakland has had thirteen straight winning seasons. Dallas has had twelve straight winning seasons. Los Angeles has had winning seasons in eleven of the last twelve years. Minnesota has had eight winning seasons out of the last nine, and were 7–7 in the other. They were all over .500 in 1978.

These are the winning organizations, representing the epitome of success in the NFL. They have gone through player changes, coaching changes, rule changes, ownership changes, a league merger and some fundamental changes in the way the game is played, and come through it all as winners. Why? Because they have a consistent philosophy toward which the entire organization is geared. I will use the single exception to prove the rule. The only losing season any of these teams experienced in the last nine years was the 1972 Rams, coached by Tommy Prothro. Prothro did not fit into the Rams organization; instead, he tried to change the organization to fit him. He made too many changes, and the Rams were not the Rams that year. As a result, they lost. When Prothro was gone, the Rams returned to their basic philosophy, and they went right back to winning. A smooth-running organization is like the human body. It rejects incompatible individuals the way the body rejects foreign tissue. You can't give a football team a heart transplant.

These four teams—the Cowboys, Rams, Vikings, and Raiders—have different philosophies. There is no single best philosophy; consistency is the key. The Cowboys have always had a complex, explosive high-risk offense. They make more mistakes than most good teams, but they make more big plays than most teams. Defensively, the Cowboys play to stop the other team from controlling the ball. They concentrate on stopping the run and the short passing game. They want an explosive game, because they figure they can "out-explode" anybody. Their defense will overcome any ball-control offense. Their offense will overcome any high-risk defense. Their philosophy makes them vulnerable to a team with an explosive, big-play offense and a conservative, "rubber-band" defense.

The Rams' philosophy is totally different. On offense, the Rams try to control the ball and minimize mistakes. They always have a "home-run" threat, like Willie Miller, to try an occasional "safe" explosion. (The long bomb is really a conservative play. The interception is the equivalent of a punt. When throwing the bomb to a speedster like Miller, the quarterback need not take a lot of time, so the risk of a sack is not that great.) Their defense is ultraconservative. They don't take risks, or concentrate on any particular aspect of the game. They think they can outplay any offense. The Rams expect to overpower the opponents offensively and defensively, or win by capitalizing on the mistakes of the opposition. The Rams' defense defeats a high-risk offense. Their offense defeats the high-risk defense. They have trouble with the "ball-control" offense, and they have trouble with a defense geared to stop the run and the long pass.

The Vikings believe in a high-risk, "anticipation" defense. They take a lot of chances, and they assume their gamble will eventually work. On the other hand, their offensive strategy is a conservative passing offense. Their backs have always been good pass receivers, and they try to get the big play by getting the ball to the backs in the open field. They throw a lot of long passes. They are not a ball-control team, but they don't take significant risks on offense. The Vikings' defense stops ball-control offenses. Their offense defeats the conservative defense. They are vulnerable to the big play on defense. Their offense can be defeated by small, quick teams.

The Raiders' defense is geared to stop the pass, in any form, and the outside run. They sacrifice size for speed and quickness on defense. On offense, they are a passing team, with a high-risk approach. Their passing attack is the most complex in football. They believe in preventing explosions and scoring quickly. On defense, they stop the big-play offense. On offense, they defeat the conservative defense and the power defense. They can be scored on by a good ball-control team. On offense, they can be stopped by the big pass rush.

Year after year, you can rely on those four teams to keep their philosophies. They draft for them, train their players for them, design their plays for them, scout for them, and play game after game without deviating from these philosophies.

This means we can count on these styles of play when handicapping these four teams. And we can count on them doing what they try to do well. The Cowboys want the ball, so they can dazzle you; the Rams play sound, conservative football; the Vikings gamble intelligently; and the Raiders believe in the power of the pass. If I see any change in those philosophies, I will bet against the team making the change consistently, until the line reflects the fall from glory.

You can see by the analysis that the Vikings should beat the Rams. They do, consistently. The Rams and Cowboys don't have an edge on each other in the match-up of styles, and they just about break even on the field. The Raiders haven't played the other three much, but they should beat Minnesota and be a toss-up with the Rams and Cowboys.

But that only accounts for four organizations. What about the other twenty-two? All the rest have failed to maintain a consistent philosophy for one reason or another. But that in itself is good betting information. Several teams have been doing well during the past few years. This could be due to the development of a basic philosophy, a coach who has a winning philosophy, or a large number of superior players. Pittsburgh, New England, Baltimore, and Cincinnati have been good teams the past few years. So has Washington.

The year 1978 was critical for the Pittsburgh Steelers. They had been good long enough to qualify as a top organization with a winning philosophy, and some of their stars were showing some age. But the Steelers were super in 1978, and definitely are on my "solid" organization list. They play a conservative power defense that controls the line of scrimmage. They believe in physical, intimidating defense, from their linemen to their defensive backs. On offense, they use power running to complement a high-risk passing offense. They run a lot of trap plays to neutralize the other team's pass rush. Their running backs are physical rather than fancy. Defensively, they are murder on small, quick teams and high-risk offenses. They are vulnerable to the conservative ball-control offense with a power fullback. On offense, they beat the run-oriented defense, or high-risk defense. They are vulnerable to a conservative defense with a good pass rush. It was obvious from their philosophy that they would give Dallas fits, which they did in the Super Bowl again in 1979.

New England is a team I don't get to see much, and they have just started to win. I will be watching them closely to see if they have become a consistent organization. Their long-range record is bad, and nobody with a spectacular record is associated with the team, so I still regard them as a poor organization.

Baltimore is a formerly successful organization that has returned to their prior formula for success. I look for them to stay a winner. Their offensive formula is centered around the all-purpose halfback and a strong passing game. They believe you win football games with offense. They play a rubber-band defense, which is conservative until the other team gets close, and then they take a lot of risks. They do well against conservative defenses, and they can contain ball-control offenses. They have trouble against quick, small defenses and the big-play offense.

Cincinnati has always had a consistent offensive philosophy, but has never stuck with one defensive philosophy. On offense, they like a power running game with a big fullback, and a high-risk, diverse passing game. This is, to me, the toughest offensive philosophy to beat, the one I would choose. To beat it, you must have a superior defensive line, and gamble, and win most of your gambles. If Cincinnati ever gets their act together defensively, watch out. As it is, they rise and fall with the level of talent they are able to get on defense. Watch their defensive statistics. In the years that they have an above-average defense, bet on them.

Washington has just lost George Allen, and my guess is he was their organization. They will undoubtedly change philosophies, become losers, and blame George. If they would stick with his approach, they could continue to win.

The rest of the teams have poor organizations that you can't count on. They rise and fall (mostly fall) on the current crop of talent, building their approach around the star players. Unfortunately, star players tend to get injured or get old. When that happens, these teams must recruit and retrain a whole new crop of stars. Often, they must also rework their strategy to suit the skills of their new stars.

And that is where the handicapping starts. Every year, I want to know how many major changes these "inconsistent" organizations have made. If they have been doing well and the changes seem inconsistent with their most recent philosophy, they are probably destined for disaster. The Colts have traded Lydell Mitchell, their all-purpose back, which could mean a change in philosophy. If they continue to use his replacement the same way they used Mitchell, then they will stay on my list of good organizations. If not, they will join the rest, and I will bet against them for a while.

If a team, like Buffalo, gets a winning coach, like Chuck Knox, analyze the players he has inherited in terms of the kind of philosophy he has used in the past. Knox is a conservative, which requires a veteran team. His quarterback needs a strong arm to throw the bombs that are a part of the Knox philosophy, and a speedy receiver to catch them. His backs must be in the "run to daylight" mold—they should follow blockers, not outrun them. His offensive line must have the experience to read defenses and take what they can get. His defense must have experience, and be steady and solid, rather than brilliant. He has the veteran line and a strong-armed quarterback, but on defense he is hurting. Unless he can trade for some veterans, he won't be an instant winner. His conservative approach should work against the weaker teams he faces, and hold its own against the mediocre high-risk offenses. Look for his teams to get wiped out by conservative ball-control teams.

If Knox changes his philosophy to match the talent available, he will turn into a loser. He must instill his philosophy into the whole organization. He could do it within two years. If he does, watch out for the Bills.

1978 is a season of changes—in most cases, changes for the worst. O.J. Simpson should ruin the 49ers, Neil Armstrong will probably undo Jack Pardee's system, Bud Wilkinson will try to learn pro football at the Cardinals' expense, et cetera.

Here are the kinds of changes I look for to predict negative results: a new head coach who has done poorly elsewhere, or hasn't been a head coach before (unless he is an assistant promoted from the ranks within the same team), college coaches, a trade for a star player who doesn't appear to fit the team's style, a lot of rookies in the starting lineup, a change of quarterbacks, or a change in the type of running backs.

Here are the kinds of changes I look for to predict positive results: trades for players who seem better equipped to fit into the team's style, changing assistant coaches in areas of weakness, or working second- and third-year men into the starting lineup.

The biggest plus a team can have going into the season is recent improvement and the willingness to stand pat, making minor changes.

Once the season starts, the number-one thing I look for is changes in basic philosophy on the part of recently successful teams. They always foretell short-term disaster.

I also look for signs of stability in philosophy for recently unsuccessful teams. This often heralds success. The two expansion teams have been very consistent so far, and, if they keep it up, they'll be winners very soon.

The factors I have discussed so far help me predict the general quality level of each team. I count on the top organizations to produce top teams. The recently successful teams may or may not stay successful, the mediocre teams can go may or may not stay successful, the mediocre teams can go either way, and the bad ones usually stay bad. Early in the season, I will bet on the basis of quality alone if I can get one of the top teams at what looks to me like a bargain. If a team has made some bad changes recently, I'll bet against them when the opposition is reasonably promising.

But my primary betting criteria are the style match-ups. On both offense and defense, a team must allow certain weaknesses to create certain strengths. An attempt to produce no weaknesses requires constantly superior personnel in every position. Occasionally, a team can field superior personnel for a year or two, but this is rare. What is normal is to make sure certain things work and hope the ability of the players is sufficient to minimize the damage in the neglected areas.

Let's discuss the possible styles of offense and defense, how to recognize them, and what the strengths and weaknesses of these styles are. On offense, these are the possible approaches.

1. The multiple, high-risk offense—as used by the Dallas Cowboys.

This offense relies on speed, skill, and finesse, at the expense of power. It is based on the theory that the longer it takes you to march down the field, the more likely you are to goof. In this offense, the plays are designed to do very well if they work, at the risk of doing very poorly if they don't. Because the multiple offense uses a wide variety of plays, the linemen must be quick. Sometimes it is necessary to sacrifice strength and size to get quickness. The backs must have the versatility to do everything, so again, power is usually sacrificed for quickness. A quarterback who can move around or has a quick release is a must, because the lack of strength hurts the pass blocking. You can recognize the multiple offense by its diversity and the scarcity of long, multiple-play drives down the field. You will see a lot of third-down, long-yardage situations, and a higher degree of success in those situations.

The strength of this offense is that it gets big yardage against mistakes. Teams that do a lot of defensive gambling get burned frequently because the wide variety of possible plays makes it difficult to guess right.

The weakness of this offense is the risk. Teams that play a conservative, low-risk defense frequently capitalize on the risk and they rarely get burned by the real "big play."

To play this offense well requires a few years' experience with it. Teams that use it can't trade much or introduce any but the most intelligent rookies into the starting lineup. This is the thinking man's offense.

2. The conservative, run-oriented offense—as typified most successfully by the Vince Lombardi Green Bay Packers.

This offense is based on the theory that you don't want to make mistakes, and that practice makes perfect. Since a team has only so much practice time available, a small number of plays are practiced over and over until they are executed to near perfection. This system does not rely on mistakes made by the other team, or on individual brilliance. The passing element is also conservative, and does not call for passing into the center of the field, where mistakes are more likely. The pass is used as support for the running game. The flankers and the tight ends must block in this offense, or one of the flankers must have blazing speed so he can consistently run his man out of the play. The backs must block for each other, and pass block, so they must be big and strong. This offense sacrifices speed and explosiveness for size and strength. The quarterback must be conservative and intelligent. He must read defenses well and rarely throw an interceptable pass. Reliability and judgment are more important than passing skills. You can recognize this offense by the type of backs that are used, the blocking rather than receiving type of tight end, the preference for the run and sideline pass, and the use of a limited variety of offensive plays. The typical scoring drive will be a multiple-play, ball-control drive, featuring the run. This team rarely faces third-down, long-yardage situations, but they'll face third-down, short-yardage situations frequently—and you can anticipate good results from them in the high-pressure, short-yardage situation.

The strength of this offense is that it is very difficult to defeat with good execution alone. Since the offense has the advantage of knowing where the ball is going, perfect execution guarantees some gain if the defense is reacting rather than anticipating. If the contest boils down to mere execution, the simple offense has a big advantage, because they have practiced their plays a good deal more than the opposing defense has practiced against them.

The weakness of this offense is its susceptibility to the high-risk defense. The lack of variety makes it easier to guess right, so a high-risk defense can win their gambles more often. And the conservative offense has difficulty making the big play required to overcome long-yardage situations.

To play this offense well requires great discipline. Brilliant but erratic players do not fit into this offense. Because of its simplicity, personnel changes are more easily made. Intelligence is important only to the quarterback. This is the "military man's" offense.

3. The conservative, pass-oriented offense—as typified by the Minnesota Vikings.

This offense is based on the theory that the linebacker cannot handle the pressure of his pass responsibilities and still stop the run, and that the short pass has the greatest potential gain with the minimum potential loss. This offense does not require a particular type of athlete in any position, except that the running backs must be able to catch the ball. The quarterback needn't be a great thrower, just quick with his release. The running element of this offense is the quick handoff, and most plays start out looking like an off-tackle play. The three options are a handoff, a short pass, or the bomb. If the linebackers play run consistently, the passing game works. If they play pass with shallow drops, the run or long pass works. If they drop back too fast, the run or the swing pass will work. This offense sacrifices the center of the field to the defense. A safe passing game must avoid the center of the field. You are watching a conservative, pass-oriented offense if: the backs catch more passes than the ends, most running plays are between the tackles, and almost all passes are toward the sidelines. This offense makes most of its first downs in two plays, and frequently gets second down ten yards to go, or second down and short yardage. It is not a good third-down offense for long or short yardage, but it's superior for third and three to eight yards.

The strength of this offense is its balance and ease of execution. It is a difficult offense to outguess or pressure into mistakes. It is the most reliable offense against weak teams. It will defeat the conservative defense with sheer skill in execution.

The defenses designed to prevent ball control—where the linemen play the run and the linebackers concentrate on the short zones—give this offense trouble. If the defense concedes the center of the field, this offense can't exploit that concession.

4. The run-oriented, high-risk offense—as typified by the Buffalo Bills, with O.J. Simpson.

This offense is designed to exploit the big-star talent. It requires very quick linemen who are exceptional run blockers. It sacrifices too much of everything. It is not a generally successful philosophy. However, when you have a great open-field runner and quick linemen, this offense works well against conservative defenses and against pass-oriented defenses. It has trouble with high-risk, run-oriented defenses.

5. The pass-oriented, high-risk offense—as typified by Oakland and Cincinnati.

This offense is based on the theory that a passing offense will get you the most points and is most difficult to defend, and that you must use the whole field to keep the pressure on the defense. Since strength and size are the key requirements for the linemen, and the fullback must have size to pass-block, it usually features a power running attack. However, Baltimore has had success with the "all-purpose" halfback as the primary running back. This offense requires an excellent passing quarterback who stays in the pocket. The tight end must have some speed. One flanker must be a real deep threat. The other must be a good pattern runner. This offense sacrifices the good outside running threat because it sacrifices speed in the line. It can utilize the speedy halfback on short passes and long passes. You can recognize this offense by the large number of passes thrown in the middle of the field, and the simplicity of the running game. This offense calls for more first-down medium to long range passes than any other. It will show a high average gain per pass completion, but very few runs from scrimmage over ten to fifteen yards.

This offense does extremely well against a run-oriented defense (or a high-risk defense) because it capitalizes on any weakness in the pass defense. It works well against zone or man-to-man coverage.

This offense is susceptible to the big-pass rush. The quarterback needs time for the patterns to develop, and to pick out secondary receivers. A defensive line that gambles a lot can give this offense trouble. Quarterback injuries or problems are death to this offense.

These are the basic offensive styles. Four of them can be made to work, year after year. The O.J. Simpson type offense is a long-run loser. That isn't to say a Simpson or Payton couldn't be fitted into any of the other styles. They both would be spectacular in the multiple offense, or even the conservative offense. In fact, the Bears are using a conservative, run-oriented offense with Payton, who is a great blocker, as well as a disciplined runner.

During most years, most teams will fit one of these patterns game after game. There will always be a few losing teams that change from game to game, and occasionally a winning team who has such superior personnel that they can get away with adapting to the defense they are playing. But, in general, the style is predictable and can help the handicapper predict the outcome.

Defenses can be broken down into several combinations. If an organization believes in winning games through defense, they will employ a high-risk defense. If they believe that defense loses games, they will employ a low-risk defense.

The high-risk defense is based on anticipation, while the low-risk defense is based on reaction. The high-risk defense creates mistakes and makes mistakes. The low-risk defense doesn't cause mistakes or make them. In general, a high-risk offense will beat a high-risk defense, and a low-risk offense will defeat the low-risk defense. How do you tell the difference between these philosophies? The high-risk defense frequently look like they know the other team's play in advance, and they make tackles the instant the ball is handed off, or before the quarterback has had time to cock his arm. By the same token, they are completely fooled more frequently, giving up big chunks of yardage. They cause more fumbles, interceptions, and losses. They give up more big plays. The low-risk defense reacts quickly, but not until there is something to react to. They don't get totally fooled much. They give up yardage a little at a time, but more consistently.

The high-risk defense requires at least a few star-quality players, and rookies fit in easier. The low-risk defense requires knowledge of the game and is played better by veterans.

The second difference is based on whether a team fears the run or the pass. If a team fears the run, they will emphasize strength and size in their defensive line. If they fear the pass, they will emphasize speed and quickness. The linemen will concentrate more on the one the team fears most. A team that gets a large number of sacks clearly fears the pass more. A team that fears the run more will stop more running plays for no gain or a loss. If a team is equally afraid of both, they will show more balance in their approach.

Finally, there is the question of power versus speed. A team that fears ball control will have bigger, more powerful linebackers. The team that fears the big play will have quicker, smaller linebackers. You can beat power with an outside running game and a good short passing game. You can beat speed with a good power-running attack.

The most common defensive combinations, and the teams that typify them, are:

1. Low-risk, balanced teams with power linebackers, as typified by the Rams. They believe in no mistakes, execution and reaction, and they don't like being beaten by power fullbacks. They are most susceptible to the conservative, short-passing game. They destroy high-risk multiple offenses and high-risk running attacks.

2. Low-risk, pass-oriented teams with quick linebackers, as typified by the Oakland Raiders. They don't like to be scored on quickly. They want to force the other team to grind out the yardage. They can be beaten by a power ball-control offense.

3. High-risk, run-oriented quick teams, like the Dallas Cowboys. They want to stop ball control and force the other team into a high-risk passing game. Run-oriented offenses and short passes just don't work against this kind of defense. High-risk pass offenses do.

4. High-risk, run-oriented power teams, like the Bears of the Dick Butkus era. They stop the run with power, the pass with anticipation. They do best against the conservative, run-oriented offense. They do poorly against the conservative, pass-oriented offense.

5. High-risk, pass-oriented power teams, like the Vikings. They stop the run with power, the pass with anticipation and a big pass rush. They are susceptible to the outside running game and the high-risk multiple offense. They stop any conservative offense.

These factors are the basis of most of my handicapping. I look for games where both the offensive and defensive style match-ups favor one team. For example, I bet the Steelers in the Super Bowl, because their wide-open passing attack figured to work against the Dallas defensive philosophy, geared to stop ball control, while Pittsburgh's power defense figured to overwhelm the smaller, quicker Cowboy offense. In addition, the Steelers had a better year statistically. So giving 3 points seemed reasonable. Fortunately, I bet early, because the line changed to 3 1/2 and 4 all over Las Vegas. Since the Steelers won by 4, getting the better line turned out to be more important than my analysis. The next chapter goes into the more specific analysis of the individual teams and their players.

8 | Handicapping the NFL—Current Strengths and Weaknesses

Once you understand the strength of each organization, their offensive and defensive philosophies, and how the different philosophies interact, you can concentrate on the strengths and weaknesses of each team in a given year.

My analysis of each team is based on what I have seen for myself, and what the statistics tell me. In addition, the rosters of the Pro Bowl teams tell me something about which teams have exceptional players. I also expect the first-round draft choice to be a quality player for most teams.

First, let's look at what you can tell from the statistics. I will do a statistical analysis of three teams based on the 1976 season: one team that had an outstanding season, the Oakland Raiders; one team that had an average season, the Chicago Bears; and one team that had a poor season, the New York Jets.

My statistics will vary slightly from the official statistics, since they are my own compilation. The NFL doesn't give permission to publish their statistics in a gambling book. They don't know which side their bread is buttered on. I don't recommend that you compile your own statistics. The NFL publishes a pocket-sized book every year that has as much in it as any other source.

Here are the statistics (from the 1976 season) that I use in analyzing a team's strengths and weaknesses, for each of the three teams.

OFFENSE	OAK	CHI	JETS	AVERAGE
Number of runs	556	578	438	
Number of passes	362	278	393	
Pct. yards run	44.0	61.5	54.5	49.8
Pct. yards pass	56.0	38.5	45.5	50.2
Pct. runs	60.5	67.5	52.7	58.5
Yards per run	4.1	4.1	4.4	4.1
Yards per pass	7.5	4.9	3.7	5.3
Pct. complete	64.2	44.2	45.8	52.2
Yards per comp.	13.8	13.9	11.0	12.7
Pct. int.	5.0	5.4	7.1	4.8
Pct. sacked	7.2	7.9	10.3	9.0
Points scored per game	25	18.1	12.1	19.2

DEFENSE				
Number of runs	479	520	582	
Number of passes	387	402	374	
Pct. yards run	43.5	47.2	52.8	49.8
Pct. yards pass	56.5	52.8	47.2	50.2
Pct. runs	55.3	56.4	60.9	58.5
Yards per run	4.0	3.8	4.5	4.1
Yards per pass	5.7	4.9	6.0	5.3
Pct. complete	50.6	49.9	54.5	52.2
Yards per comp.	14.5	13.1	12.1	12.7
Pct. int.	4.1	5.9	2.8	4.8
Pct. sacked	10.6	10.9	4.1	9.1
Points allowed per game	17.0	15.4	27.3	19.2
Composite record of opponents	92–90	104–75–3	95–87	

First, let's look at the Oakland offense. Since they were 13–1, they played a lot of kill-the-clock offense, which will cause an increase in the number of runs, and a decrease in the yards gained per run. This explains their slightly high percentage of runs. Their yardage gained shows a marked edge to passing yards. They throw a few more interceptions than average, but they get a huge average yards per pass. Their completion average is remarkable considering the average yards per completion. They protect the quarterback well and score a lot of points. My summary of their offense is: respectable running game, exceptional passing game with strong short passing producing high completion percentage, and good long and intermediate passing producing a high average gain per completion. They should score a lot of points against any team with a poor pass defense, and a reasonable number of points against anything but a superior pass defense.

The Oakland defense faced a lot of catch-up football due to the 13–1 record. This explains the large amount of passing done against them, and the high yards per completion. However, their low interception percentage is a sign of weakness, in view of those circumstances. They are average against the run. My summary of their defense is: basically average on defense, with a possible vulnerability to the bomb. They could have trouble against good offensive teams.

Overall betting summary: They look like they could give a lot of points (on the spread) to a team with a poor pass defense and a poor offense. They should beat average defenses by 7 to 10 points unless they face a superior offense. In view of their superior passing attack, I wouldn't give them points unless they played a team with a great pass defense on the road, and then I wouldn't give them over 3 points. If I could get more than 7 points with a team with a good ball-control offense and long-pass threat, I would take the points.

To bet on Oakland, you will almost always give points. You will probably never get points at home, and rarely over 3 points on the road. Let's look at the different ranges of point spreads, and assume the relative quality of their opponent and location of the game indicate the point spread is about right.

Oakland—14 points or more. I would bet on them only at home against a team with no pass defense, no-better-than-mediocre run offense, a poor sack record on offense and defense, and no long passing game. I would bet against them if their opponent had an above average pass defense and did not allow their quarterback to be sacked more than 10 percent. If the game was not at Oakland, I could take the points even with a lot of sacks.

Oakland—11–14 points. I could bet Oakland against a team with a below average pass defense and average or worse offense. I could bet them against an average pass defense and very poor offense. I could bet against Oakland if a team had an above average pass defense and good long-passing threat.

Oakland—8–10 points. I could bet Oakland against any team with a below average pass defense. I could bet against Oakland with a team with a superior pass defense, or above average pass defense with a lot of sacks, and a good passing offense.

Oakland—4–7 points. I could bet Oakland against any team with an average pass defense. I could bet against them with a team with a superior pass defense and a good pass offense.

Oakland—0–3 points. I could bet Oakland against a team with an average pass offense, unless they had a superior pass defense and a lot of interceptions. I could bet against Oakland with a team that was superior in all phases of defense, especially sacks, and had a good long passing offense.

Oakland plus anything. I would bet them against any team except the other four top organizations. Those four could only give Oakland points at home in an off year for Oakland.

Now let's look at the Bears. The Bear offense is truly run-oriented, due more to an inept passing attack than an overwhelming running attack. Their average yards per carry is only average, but that isn't too bad considering the lack of a passing attack. They do have a long threat, as indicated by the average gain per completion. My summary of their offense is: all run, no pass. They could beat teams with a weakness against the run, but a good run defense might shut them out. A weak pass defense is almost no liability against them.

On defense, the Bears are very strong in all departments. They get a lot of interceptions and sacks, which helps their offense get points. They are above average in all defensive departments. My summary of the Bear defense is: a sound defense that you must out-execute to beat. Could be a high-risk defense in view of sacks, interceptions, and high yardage per completion.

Overall summary: the Bears played a treacherous schedule and still played solid defense. The offense is the key to betting the Bears. They should beat teams you can run against, get beat by teams you can't run against. They are a solid, but not great team. You couldn't give them more than eleven or twelve points, nor could they give more than eleven or twelve. I would hesitate to give them points with a team that was not outstanding against the run. I couldn't bet the Bears giving points on the road to any but the poorer teams, and it would be hard to give more than a touchdown to anyone, even at home.

If the point spread on a Bear game seemed reasonable in terms of quality, I would bet the Bears if the other team was below average against the run, their opponents if they were above average against the run. The Bears do not represent a complex betting problem.

The Jets had a run-oriented offense that was forced to pass because they got behind all the time. A low completion percentage and low yards per completion is a disaster. Their running average was good, but that could be due to going against a lot of prevent defenses. My summary is: They are awful once they get behind. You could expect any good defense against the run to stop them cold.

The Jets' defense against the run is so poor, and their sacks so low, that they must have a horrendous defensive line. With so little help from the line, the secondary must be decent, because the completion percentage isn't all that high considering the low average yards per completion. My summary is: The Jets are extremely susceptible to ball control, on the ground or with short passes. A team that throws a lot of deep stuff might have trouble with them.

Overall summary: The Jets are clearly a poor team, and could give points only to a team with no running game at all and a poor run defense, and then not very many points. A good ball-control team with a tough run defense should beat them by 20+ points.

If the line on a Jets game seemed reasonable, I would bet the Jets if the other team had a pass-oriented offense with a low completion percentage and high yards per completion, and a weak run defense. I would bet any ball control team with a good run defense and high sack or interception percentage. As bad as the Jets are, I wouldn't give them more than 14 points at home.

Based on the analysis of each team's weaknesses, I look at the college draft to see if a team tried to help itself in a weak area. Oakland looked like they had secondary problems, so I would expect them to draft a defensive back right away. Sure enough, their first pick (on the second round) was Mike Davis, a defensive back from Colorado.

The Bears needed to help their passing game, but they didn't draft a receiver until the seventh round. A bad sign, in my opinion.

The hapless Jets needed passing and defensive linemen most of all, and that's what they drafted for: wide receivers and defensive linemen on six of their first seven picks.

The analysis of each team should include an evaluation of the potential for improvement from first- and second-year men, such as Walter Payton and Bob Avellini of the Bears, or age in key positions, like Willie Brown of Oakland. The Bears, in general, had a young team, so improvement was likely, though they drafted poorly. Oakland has quite a bit of age on offense, so they could drop off a bit. The Jets were rebuilding without Namath, so anything was possible, but rapid improvement seemed unlikely. With their good draft, they looked as if they might perk up a bit in 1978 or 1979.

Looking at the Pro Bowl is interesting. Oakland had four offensive players on the team: two receivers, Branch and Kasper; and the left guard and tackle, Art Shell and Gene Upshaw. If Oakland lined up strong left, these four men would be the four guys outside the center on the left side of the field. Given that Ken Stabler would have been the Pro Bowl quarterback were it not for an injury (and that he is left-handed), you have a pretty good idea why it is tough to stop the Oakland passing game. The only Oakland defensive player to make the Pro Bowl was Phil Villapiano, a linebacker.

The Bears' Pro Bowl representatives were Payton and Wally Chambers, the Bears' super-defensive tackle. Chambers had knee surgery following the Pro Bowl. Losing a player like Chambers might turn the Bears' solid defense into a mediocre one. (As it turned out, that was the case.) The Jets didn't get a single player in the Pro Bowl.

I do the above analysis for each team before the season starts. Once the season begins, I watch the weekly statistics for improvement or deterioration in each department. I continually update my team profiles as to general ability, style, and strengths and weaknesses.

Then I watch every game on the boob tube. I am looking for several things when I watch a game, all of which help handicap future games. The first thing I watch closely are the kicking teams. I don't like to see rookies as kick returners unless they also play offensively or defensively, at least part-time. If a guy has only a few opportunities per game to show his ability, he will take too many chances and be too uptight. Over the years, I have seen too many games lost by rookies on kick returns fumbling or making serious judgment errors. I rate a rookie return man as a negative one point on the point spread.

If I see a return man with good hands and a good first move, who carries the ball tucked in instead of like a loaf of bread, that's worth 1/2 point, and if he seems to have exceptional open field ability, another 1/2 point.

Defensively, I like to see the same guy pressuring the return—if not making the tackle—on punts and kickoffs. The best weapon against the kick return is the freelance man with good instincts and lots of guts. He will cause mistakes often, and hold the return to short yardage most of the time. If a team has a real good kick coverer, that's worth 1/2 point. On the negative side, I don't like to see the first couple of guys downfield overrun the play without at least causing the return man to alter course. If that happens too often, I take off 1/2 point. If the kick coverage teams miss a lot of tackles, that's 1/2 point to the bad.

All these things require seeing a whole game, and preferably two. The announcers will sometimes give you some information in this area. Statistics don't help much, because field position affects punt returns so much and kickoffs can't be judged unless you know how deep the kickoff went. A thirty-yard return is one thing from the end zone, another from the fifteen-yard line.

The next thing I watch is the line play. In particular, I look for consistent double-teaming of one defensive lineman. This can mean one of two things: The offensive lineman getting help is a weak player, or the lineman being double-teamed is a superior player. Blocking assignments being as complex as they are, you can usually tell which is the case, because the potentially weak lineman will occasionally have a different man as his assignment. If they help him with a double team, then, too, he is a weak link. Otherwise, a superior defensive lineman is the reason for the double team.

A weak blocker is a detriment more to the pass than the run, because you can always run away from the weakness, but the passing pocket must be protected from all sides. If I see a weak blocker, then any team with two strong players playing next to each other, and one of them opposite the weak link, is going to give that weak man fits.

A superior defensive lineman is murder on the pass block-ing. He can "make" a defense when he is opposite anything but a superior blocker. On the other hand, if he is neutralized or injured, the effect can be devastating, since his teammates get accustomed to his absorbing the pressure for them. When I identify such a player, he frequently becomes the key to my analysis of a game. Can he be neutralized? Or will he require constant double-teaming? Wally Chambers had a year in 1976 where he was double-teamed nearly every game. For years, Alan Page was such a lineman. Paul Smith of Denver was that good for a few years. These players became crucial to their teams' defensive performance in many games.

The next thing I look for in line play is the direction of their run in short yardage situations, and on first down deep in their own territory. They will run toward their best blockers 80 to 90 percent of the time. The Miami Dolphins ran to the right over and over in their championship years. Right over Larry Little's position. The Vikings ran toward Ed White and Ron Yary, and the Raiders behind Shell and Upshaw.

You also judge the defense's effectiveness at stopping the run toward each side of the field. If there is a situation in which a team prefers running in the direction where the defense has shown strength, they could be in trouble, and vice versa. Injuries to defensive players are more critical if they are going to cause substitutes to face the team's strong side. Injuries to offensive linemen on the team's preferred side are more critical.

The individual match-ups I consider to be the most critical in all of football are the offensive guards against the defensive tackles. If a team comes up with a great player in any of these positions, you can expect them to be above their norm for the length of time the player is great. Larry Little was the best offensive guard I have ever seen, and the MVP on the Dol-phins, as far as I was concerned. As soon as I saw him, I knew the Dolphins were in for some great years. Jerry Kramer was the key to the Packers. Joe Greene made the Iron Curtain iron, and the Steelers champs. Bob Lilly was the key to the Dallas defense. Now the Cowboys have Randy White, who may be the best of them all. Alan Page, Gene Upshaw, and Merlin Olson were other great ones.

The offensive guards and defensive tackles control the game because they control the center of the field. Since football is strategically similar to a chess game, you know (if you are a chess player) that it is essential to control the center. Find a player who can control the center of the field, and you can pick up some money betting his team.

How do you recognize a great player? He consistently dominates his man, no matter what his assignment is, and he never stops trying until the whistle blows. If he is on offense, he will rarely need double-team help. If he is on defense, he will constantly get double-teamed. He will frequently carry a player whose position is next to his to the Pro Bowl with him. If one of these superstars is hurt, be careful of betting his team.

The linebackers are the glamour boys of the defense. They get to do all the spectacular things, like make the most of the tackles. I don't like spectacular linebackers; I like reliable ones. I don't care how many tackles he makes, so long as plays in his territory don't go too far. Linebacking is a positional responsibility. Each man has a territory to protect. I look for a linebacker who is always there when the play comes his way, and makes the tackle consistently in his area. A linebacker must be smart, and a good tackler. A weak middle linebacker means trouble against a ball-control team. Weak outside linebackers mean trouble against teams that sweep a lot, or throw to their backs a lot.

Cornerbacks are there for everyone to see. A weak one gets thrown at a lot. Good ones don't. A team covers for a weak cornerback by helping him with the free safety. If you see the free safety consistently on one side of the field, it's probably due to the weakness of the cornerback. You can win bets just because you know a great receiver is going to be working against a weak cornerback all day. If a team's best receiver is going to be covered by a great cornerback and his team is susceptible to sacks, this can be reason enough to make a bet, everything else being equal. I won many a bet because I knew Jimmy Johnson of the 49ers could blanket his man, stymieing a particular team's passing attack.

Finally, we have the offensive heroes, the guys the cameras follow all over the place: quarterbacks, running backs and receivers. The statistics on these guys basically tell the story.

The only thing I look for, other than the obvious, is a player so good he overcomes his teammates' failings consistently. Joe Namath, in his glory years, made stars out of a bunch of average receivers. He was so accurate they just needed to be open a smidgen and he would get the ball to them. Fran Tarkenton has such phenomenal instincts he consistently overcomes bad pass blocking with his elusiveness. The younger Roger Staubach turned good pass coverage into ten-yard gains by running himself. Walter Payton turns three-yard gains into thirty-yard gains by fighting out of tackles. Larry Csonka runs through tacklers who didn't get blocked. Biletnikoff catches bad passes.

Players like these represent dangers to other analyses. The great players at the skill positions unpredictably overcome team inferiorities. The Jets' Super Bowl win was that kind of event. You can't really tell when a star is going to glitter. So I am a little wary of betting on the basis of an analysis that could be overcome by a truly remarkable player. If I don't think a team will beat the spread if they don't stop a player of this caliber, I don't bet. If my primary basis for betting is a team's ability to rush Tarkenton, forget it. They may defeat the blocking and never lay a finger on him. But if I don't expect that, and want to bet against the Vikings, I bet.

Finally, I watch a game for "near misses" and luck. Things like receivers who get five yards behind everyone, but then drop the ball; or runners slipping with an open field in front of them, or penalties on touchdown plays. If a team overcomes these kinds of things and still beats the spread, that is a big plus. If they win because of the breaks, that is a big minus. You can make a lot of money betting against teams that have won a couple of games on luck they didn't create, or betting on teams who have been winning in spite of bad luck. I don't like to bet on teams that have been losing on bad breaks because they begin to expect them, and it becomes a self-fulfilling prophecy.

That about sums it up. My analysis is consistently trying to find strength against weakness. Whether it be in basic philosophies, team statistics, or individual player match-ups, I want to exploit situations where strength will overcome weakness.

To illustrate how I use all this information, let's handicap a hypothetical game between Oakland and the Bears, as the first game of the 1977 season. (I hate to use a real game, because it is so phony to pick one that fits all your theories perfectly.)

First, let's look at how many points we can expect the Bears to get against Oakland. Oakland's basic defensive philosophy didn't work for them in 1976. Teams passed well against them. But they drafted a cornerback, and have a history of making their pass defense work. I expect them to improve at least a little on pass defense. The Bears did little to help their pass offense, but Avellini got in a good solid year, and should improve. They drafted an offensive tackle number one, and he made the team. In addition, Payton is going into his third year, and should reach his peak, so I expect a slight improvement in their passing game, and a little more improvement in their running game.

With these factors in mind, let's look at the statistics. Remember, the Bears played a nasty schedule in 1976, while Oakland had a normal schedule. The Bears are a running team, and run pretty well. Oakland is slightly above average against the run. The Bears' only passing threat is the long pass to James Scott, who averaged almost twenty yards per catch. Oakland is vulnerable to the long pass. You would expect the match-ups to favor the Bears' offense somewhat. So the Bears, especially in view of their probable improvement and tougher schedule, should score a bit over their average of 18 points—about 20 to 21 points. However, the Bears like to run to their right, and that's where Villapiano plays (left linebacker), and he was a Pro Bowler. This is somewhat offset by the fact that left cornerback was the Raiders' weak spot, and the place where they could stick the rookie, so Villapiano has to be conscious of his pass drops to help the rookie. But the Bears don't have a short to medium passing game, so I figure Villapiano will hurt the Bears' running game a little. Call it 20 points for the Bears.

Now let's see what the Raiders should get. They had a phenomenal offensive year in '76. They are getting a little age on offense, but not much. Still, I wouldn't look for them to be quite as good, but a great pass-oriented offense, nonetheless. The Bears, on the other hand, are going without Chambers, a true superstar in 1976. This should seriously hurt their pass rush, since Chambers was their sack leader. In fact, they could easily slip to a below-average pass defense team without Chambers. Also, they didn't draft for defense, so I expect them to be significantly worse.

Remembering these things, plus the difficulty of the Bears' schedule, let's look at the statistics. The Bears play the run well, and Oakland is average on running. The Bears rushed the passer, held down completions, and got a lot of interceptions in 1976. That was with Chambers. They might stay tough against the run without him, though not as tough, but against the pass they should be about average. I would say Oakland should score a few less points than their average against the Bears, say 23 points. But the Raiders run to their left, as a rule. Waymond Bryant is the Bears' right linebacker, and he has a tendency to get out of position. In addition, the Raiders throw to their left a lot, and that is the soft spot in the Bear defense. Allan Ellis, the Bears' best cornerback, is on the other side. Also, Upshaw is a superstar, Shell made the Pro Bowl, and they are both on the Bears' soft side. Let's make it 25 points for Oakland.

The kicking games are about equal. They both cover kicks

very well; the Bears are a better return team, but Ray Guy is the premiere punter in the NFL. The placekickers are both a little below average.

So our basic quality spread is Oakland by 5 points. Give them another point because of a superior organization, and make it 6. If the game were at Oakland, my point spread would be Oakland by 9 1/2 points. If it were in Chicago, I would make Oakland a 2 1/2 point favorite. The home-field advantage is worth 3 1/2 points in pro football.

The basic philosophies of the teams match up well for the Bears. But I would be afraid of the loss of Chambers. I would only bet this game if I got a 3-point variation in the spread, from my spread. In other words, I could bet Oakland at home giving 6 1/2, or in Chicago getting 1/2. I could bet the Bears in Oakland getting 12 1/2, or at home getting 5 1/2.

That's how I handicap the National Football League. Then I hope that the referees only see the other side holding, that my team's punts bounce out of bounds on the one-yard line, and that it is the other guy's quarterback who gets hurt in the first quarte.r It doesn't always work out that way, but I'm right in the analysis often enough to overcome the 11–10 price, with something to spare for my safe-deposit box.

9 | My Football System

I started working on this system in 1966, as soon as I had learned enough about computers to apply them to the problem. Football was a natural thing to try because of the relatively small amount of information available on each game. The first system was actually for college football, and involved a complicated program that took so long when it ran on the computer that I stopped the computer, thinking it had gone into a loop. After looking at the information inside the computer (you can do this by means of something called a "core dump," which is a printout of everything in the computer's memory), I decided the program just wasn't done yet, so I started it again. After forty-five minutes, it printed out a prediction on every college game on which a line was available for that Saturday. This was at about seven in the morning on Saturday. By then, I had been awake for twenty-four hours and was exhausted, so I didn't take my usual precautions to check if the program had functioned properly. I just decided to bet anyway.

I took the ten games where the computer prediction varied most from the point spread. I bet ten bucks a game, a big bet for me at the time. If I lost all ten games, that would have been $110, a week's salary. I wasn't too sensible a bettor then.

Anyway, nine out of the ten teams won. I was ecstatic. It seemed like the big breakthrough. That Sunday I went to the office to double-check all my keypunching, and I found an error, which I corrected, taking the mispunched card from the middle of the deck, and putting it back at the end of the deck. Then I ran the program again, just to see if the minor change would affect the predictions. Every prediction changed by several points. The program had a bug (a malfunction) that caused the predictions to depend on the order in which the cards were entered. I had won nine out of ten on the basis of a programming mistake!

Eventually, I fixed the program and reran it. This time the top ten picks went 5 and 5. My exhilaration evaporated. The program wound up losing a little money for the remainder of the season, so I spent the next few months playing around with the information I had gathered. Finally, I developed a technique that seemed to work for the colleges, but not for the pros. For the next three seasons, the computer picked 63 percent winners versus the point spread on college football. Then it suddenly stopped working. It picked 49 percent the next year, so I made some changes and it picked 47 percent the next year. I gave up on college football and started concentrating on the pros. I stuck to the basic concept of the college system, with a couple of major modifications, and by 1969 the program started winning. Nothing spectacular, but it was picking 55 percent winners and betting over half the games. In 1970, I didn't have access to a computer for part of the season, so I devised a manual technique to accomplish roughly what the computer had been doing. The changes necessary to accommodate a "human computer" actually helped, and my percentage went up to 57 percent. I have been using the technique ever since. Oddly enough, 1974, the first big baseball year, was my only losing year with the football system. My win percentage of 53 percent in 1977 was also a disappointment. But the overall record since 1969 is 318 wins, 249 losses and 22 ties, a win percent of 56 percent. This is not a spectacular percentage, but if you are a thousand-dollar bettor, it is enough to win you an average of five or six thousand a year. Since it involves around thirty to forty hours of work a season, I consider it worthwhile.

Let's start with the facts behind the technique. If a team loses a fumble or has a pass intercepted, this is equivalent to losing twenty-five yards of offense, and giving the other team twenty-five yards of offense, on the average. This fact resulted from a regression analysis I did, with the help of a statistician. Since I don't understand regression analysis, I can't explain it to you, but he guaranteed me it works. Since the figure makes sense to me and the technique works, I use it.

Fumbles and interceptions are less predictable than yards gained. If a team fumbles twice a game for five games, that doesn't tell you much about the sixth game. If a team gains one hundred yards running for five games, it tells you a lot about the sixth game. In fact, past fumbles and interceptions are about 20 percent as predictive as yards gained. (Thank the regression analysis for this figure.)

The home-team advantage, based on an analysis of the past ten years, is worth 3 1/2 points. (This discounts meaningless games and playoff games. The home advantage is less in those games).

But the football system can't be applied to year-old statistics (unlike my baseball system), and you won't have enough information to make systematic football bets until five games into the current season. Depending on what gets printed in your local newspaper, you should be able to glean the necessary statistics from the game summaries in your local newspaper, but in some localities (where the game summaries are sketchy) you'll have to resort to *The Gold Sheet* or *Pro Football News*.

The logic behind the system is this: You want to adjust each team's performance based on the quality of the opposition they have faced. Then you want to use the individual factors to predict how a team will do, category by category. Finally, you want to convert the category predictions into a prediction of the final outcome. In order to set up your football system you'll need the following information (these statistics are totals to date for the whole regular season):

1. Points scored
2. Points allowed
3. Rushing yardage
4. Rushing yardage allowed
5. Passing yardage
6. Passing yardage allowed
7. Fumbles lost
8. Opponents' fumbles recovered
9. Interceptions thrown
10. Interceptions made
11. Penalties against
12. Penalties for

When I use the computer, I include statistics on kick returns, but this makes the amount of work nearly impossible. In any case, it seems to make very little difference in the results.

If you don't have access to any of this information, just leave it out. If your newspaper doesn't keep track of it for you, you will have to keep running totals of the information for every team.

The first step in the system is to try to minimize distortions in the raw statistics. The biggest cause of distortion is the weather. Terrible weather inhibits the offense. Newspaper accounts of a game will usually tell you if the weather was especially bad. Given good weather, teams average around 630 total yards gained between them, and around 39 points. Teams average about twenty-five passes each per game. If you know the weather was bad for a game and the statistics are substantially lower than the averages here, adjust them. If the total yards are low by 30 percent, raise each team's passing and/or rushing yards by 30 percent. If the teams hardly passed at all, just raise the passing yards for both teams. Use your judgment as to whether or not to raise the passing or running yards. You won't mess things up if you are a little wrong, as long as you make the same percentage adjustment to each team's total yards. If the total yardage for a bad-weather game is low, the total scoring will probably be low as well—you must raise the points along with the yardage. For every thirteen yards added to a team's total yardage, you must add one point.

The second kind of distortion we need to minimize is the effect on statistics in a runaway. I define a runaway as a game in which one team is ahead by 21 points going into the fourth quarter, and 17 or more total points were scored in the fourth quarter without the trailing team ever getting within 14 points. In these games, the fourth quarter frequently turns into an offensive circus, and statistics get inflated. In a runaway, reduce the number of points scored in the fourth quarter for both teams proportionately, until you get down to a total of 14 points. Then reduce the passing yardage of each team by ten yards for every point subtracted, and the running yardage by three yards for every point subtracted. (Most of the late fireworks are caused by passing).

The final distortion to be eliminated is the effect of a key injury. For an injury to rate as a key injury, the player must be of all-pro caliber, or the number-one quarterback. The very best quarterbacks, such as Bert Jones or Terry Bradshaw, are worth three points. The best running backs, like Walter Payton or Earl Campbell, are worth three points. A great lineman, like John Hannah, is worth two points. You will have to use your judgment in deciding how much a player is worth. Add or subtract the points, depending on the player's position, only if his team lost to the point spread (obviously you must record the point spread for every game). For every point you add or subtract, you must adjust the yardage by thirteen yards. For example, if a quarterback was hurt, you add three points and thirty-nine passing yards to his team's total statistics.

Once your individual raw statistics are adjusted for these "abnormal" factors, you are ready to convert the total statistics mathematically—using the system. I will give you a step-by-step description, with an explanation of what is being accomplished. At the end of the chapter, there are examples of the steps.

The first thing we must do is adjust the statistics for teams that have played more than half their games at home, or vice versa. The things we wish to adjust are the rushing and passing yards, offensively and defensively. (Categories 3–6 in the preceding list.) The home team has an 8-percent advantage. This procedure adjusts for that advantage. (Note: The following step numbers within the instructions relate to Table 1 on page 46.)

Step 1. Divide each of the four yardage categories by the number of games a team has played.

Step 2. Multiply each result by the number of excess games a team has played at home or on the road. (If a team has played five home games and three road games, multiply by 2). Multiply each result by .08. That will give the amount by which you want to adjust each category.

Step 3. If the team has had an excess of home games, you subtract from the offensive statistics and add to the defensive statistics. You do the opposite if they've had more road games.

The next thing we want to do is establish two statistics: a team's ability to convert yards to points and its ability to stop other teams from converting yards to points. We need to establish a predictive statistic for yards gained which reflects running and passing yards as well as penalty yards and turnovers. A turnover has the value of fifty yards. The following steps will get us the offensive and defensive effectiveness of a team with respect to yards versus points.

Step 4. Add together adjusted rushing and passing yards, giving you yards gained.

Step 5. Add together rushing yards allowed and passing yards allowed, giving you yards allowed.

Step 6. Compare penalties for (12) and against (11). Subtract the smaller number from the larger number and divide by 2. We want to assign half the excess penalty yards to the offense, half to the defense.

Step 7. If penalty yards against (11) were higher, subtract the result of Step 6 from the yards gained, and add the result of Step 6 to yards allowed. If penalty yards against were lower, do the opposite.

Step 8. Get the team's net turnovers by adding "fumbles lost" (7) and "had intercepted" (9), and comparing them to the sum of "fumbles recovered" (8) and "intercepted" (10). Subtract the smaller total from the larger, and multiply by 25. We want to assign twenty-five yards to the offense and twenty-five yards to the defense for each excess turnover.

Step 9. If a team benefited from more turnovers than they made—if "(8) + (10)" is greater than "(7) + (9)"—add the result of Step 8 to yards gained and subtract the result of Step 8 from yards allowed. Do the opposite if they turned the ball over more than they took it away.

Step 10. Now we have total yards gained and allowed. Divide points scored (1) by yards gained (Step 9). This gives the "OER" (offensive effectiveness ratio).

Step 11. Divide points allowed by yards allowed. This gives the "DER" (Defensive Effectiveness Ratio).

The next thing we must do is adjust the key statistics based on the level of competition each team has faced. To do this, first we must establish what is average for each of the key categories, rushing yards, passing yards, rushing yards allowed, passing yards allowed, OER (Offensive Effectiveness Ratio, and DER (Defensive Effectiveness Ratio).

Step 12. For each key statistic, get the league total by adding the total for each of the teams, then dividing by the number of teams to get the average for each category.

Now we are ready to adjust the key statistics based on the level of competition.

Step 13. For each category for each team, add together the totals of the teams they have played. If they have played a team twice, add that team's total twice. Divide this sum by the number of games played. Divide this result by the league average for the category. This gives you the opposition's ratio of the average.

Step 14. We use this ratio to adjust the opposite figure for the team we are adjusting. For example, the competition level of the opponents for yards rushing allowed is used to adjust yards rushing, and vice versa. So, for each category, divide the team's total by the ratio for the opposite figure. (If a team has, for example, been playing teams that are below average in rushing defense, we want to reduce their yards rushing).

Now every key statistic has been adjusted for the level of competition. I take it one step further, and adjust for the level of competition the competition has faced.

Step 15. We recompute the league average for each category. (Due to rounding error, we must do this for both offense and defense).

Step 16. Same as Step 13, except using the adjusted totals and averages. Now we have the average level of the competition adjusted for *their* competition.

Step 17. We get our final adjusted total by dividing the team's original totals in each key category by the adjusted ratio obtained in Step 15 for the opposite category. (The OER by DER, DER by OER, et cetera.)

We are now ready to predict the total yardage for each team in each category. Here is where we use each team's defensive ability to predict how many yards their opponents will gain.

Step 18. Divide the opponent's final adjusted rushing yards allowed, and passing yards allowed, by the league averages for those categories. Multiply the result by the team in question's final adjusted total in the corresponding offensive category. (Opponent's rushing yards allowed divided by league average multiplied by final adjusted rushing yards). Divide this result by the number of games played, and you have the predicted offensive yards rushing and passing for both teams.

Now we want to adjust the predicted total yards by the predicted turnover deficit, or advantage.

Step 19. First, we want to know what the average number of turnovers is per team. To get this figure, we add all the fumbles lost and passes intercepted for all the teams, divide by the number of teams, and divide by the number of weeks in the season, so far. This gives you the average number of turnovers per team, per game.

Step 20. Now we want to get each team's number of turnovers per game. Divide total turnovers (fumbles lost plus passes intercepted) by games played. Remembering that turnovers are only 20 percent as predictive as other statistics, we multiply the league average by 4, add a team's average turnovers, and divide by 5. This gives you their predicted turnovers. Repeat this process on the turnovers caused, using fumbles recovered and passes intercepted, to get a team's predicted turnovers received.

Step 21. By looking at each team's predicted turnovers, we can see which team has the advantage in this area, and how many more turnovers they should get. Add each team's turnovers to their opponent's turnovers received. The team with the lower number has the advantage. Subtract the lower number from the higher number. Multiply the result by 25. Add the result to the total yardage of the team with the turnover advantage. Subtract the same amount from the total yardage of their opponent.

Now we have the final predicted total yardage for each team, which we can use to predict the score of the game on a neutral field.

Step 22. Take each team's final adjusted DER and divide it by the average DER for the league. Multiply the result by the opposition's final OER. This gives you the opposition's predicted ability to convert yards to points. Multiply the total yards predicted (adjusted for turnovers) by the predicted ability to convert yards to points, and presto, you have the predicted points scored.

Step 23. Finally, add 3 1/2 points to the home team's predicted score. You have the predicted final score; and therefore, the predicted point spread. I bet all games where the predicted point spread is different from the real point spread by three or more points. On overs and unders, I bet if the difference is five or more points. (I have only been betting these for two years, with 57-percent winners, staying away from the bad weather areas after Thanksgiving).

One last betting rule. I never bet a game after Thanksgiving weekend if both teams are mathematically eliminated from the playoffs.

Examples, step by step. Here are four hypothetical teams who have played five games each. They have each played the other twice, except A and B and C and D have only played once. Our job is to predict the point spread for Team A playing at Team B and Team C playing at Team D. Teams A and D have played three home games, Teams B and C, two. Here are their season's statistics, pre-adjusted for weather, injuries, and runaways:

TABLE I

		TEAM A	TEAM B	TEAM C	TEAM D
1	Points	101	98	62	134
2	Points allowed	94	142	82	77
3	Rushing	740	710	630	830
4	Allowed	710	860	730	610
5	Passing	770	700	660	800
6	Allowed	760	710	720	740
7	Fumbles lost	10	15	8	8
8	Fumbles gained	12	6	8	15
9	Int.	12	10	4	11
10	Int. by	7	9	8	13
11	Pen.	300	210	180	460
12	Opp. pen.	280	270	290	330

Step 1. Get yardage per game.

	TEAM A	TEAM B	TEAM C	TEAM D	
3	148	142	126	166	(830/5 = 166)
4	142	172	146	122	(610/5 = 122)
5	154	140	132	160	(800/5 = 160)
6	152	142	144	148	(740/5 = 148)

Step 2. Get adjustment factor for excess of home or road games. (Teams A and D have 3 home, 2 road, while B and C have 3 road, 2 home.)

	TEAM A	TEAM B	TEAM C	TEAM D	
3	12	11	10	13	$(166 \times 1 \times .08 = 13)$
4	11	14	12	10	$(122 \times 1 \times .08 = 10)$
5	12	11	11	13	$(160 \times 1 \times .08 = 13)$
6	12	11	12	12	$(148 \times 1 \times .08 = 12)$

Step 3. Adjust total yards for excess of home or road games.

	TEAM A	TEAM B	TEAM C	TEAM D	
3	728	721	640	817	$(830 - 13 = 817)$
4	721	846	718	620	$(610 + 10 = 620)$
5	758	711	671	787	$(800 - 13 = 787)$
6	772	699	708	752	$(740 + 12 = 752)$

Steps 4 and 5. Get yards gained and yards allowed for each team.

	TEAM A	TEAM B	TEAM C	TEAM D	
Yards gained	1486	1432	1311	1604	$(817 + 787 = 1604)$
Allowed	1493	1545	1426	1372	$(620 + 752 = 1372)$

Step 6. Get penalty differential.

A	B	C	D	
+10	−30	−55	+65	(460−330=130/2=65)

Step 7. Adjust yards gained and allowed for penalties.

	A	B	C	D	
Gained	1476	1462	1366	1539	(1604−65=1539)
Allowed	1503	1515	1371	1437	(1372+65=1437)

Step 8. Get turnover yards.

A	B	C	D	
+75	+250	−100	−225	[(15 + 13) − (8 + 11)] × 25 = 225

Step 9. Adjust yards gained and allowed for turnovers.

	A	B	C	D	
Gained	1401	1212	1466	1764	(1539+225=1764)
Allowed	1578	1765	1271	1212	(1437−225=1212)

Steps 10 and 11. Get offensive and defensive effectiveness ratios.

	A	B	C	D	
OER	.072	.081	.042	.076	(134/1764 = .076)
DER	.060	.080	.065	.064	(77/1212 = .064)

eague average for each "key" statistic.
Note: The league OER and DER are equal.

OER-DER	.068	([.072+.081+.042+.076]/4 = .068)
Rushing	727.5	([740+710+630+830]/4 = 727.5)
Passing	732.5	([770+700+660+800]/4 = 732.5)

Step 13. Get the level of competition in the form of a ratio for each key statistic.

	A	B	C	D	
OER	.93	.91	1.12	1.02	(.072 + .072 + .081 + .081 + .042) ÷ 5 ÷ .068 = 1.02
DER	.99	.94	1.01	1.01	(.060 + .060 + .080 + .080 + .065) ÷ 5 ÷ .068 = 1.01
Rushing	1.00	1.00	1.02	.97	(728 + 728 + 721 + 721 + 640) ÷ 5 ÷ 727.5 = .97
Allowed	.97	.93	1.03	1.06	(721 + 721 + 846 + 846 + 718) ÷ 5 ÷ 727.5 = 1.06
Passing	.99	1.00	1.02	.99	(758 + 758 + 711 + 711 + 671) ÷ 5 ÷ 732.5 = .99
Allowed	.99	1.01	1.01	1.00	(772 + 772 + 699 + 699 + 708) ÷ 5 ÷ 732.5 = 1.00

Step 14. Adjust totals based on the competition.

	A	B	C	D	
OER	.073	.086	.041	.075	$(.076 \div 1.01 = .075)$
DER	.065	.088	.058	.063	$(.064 \div 1.02 = .063)$
Rushing	751	775	621	771	$(817 \div 1.06 = 771)$
Allowed	721	846	704	639	$(620 \div .97 = 639)$
Passing	766	704	664	787	$(787 \div 1.00 = 787)$
Allowed	780	699	694	760	$(752 \div .99 = 760)$

Step 15. Recompute the league averages, based on the adjusted totals.

OER	.069	$(.073 + .086 + .041 + .075) \div 4 = .069$
DER	.069	$(.065 + .088 + .058 + .063) \div 4 = .069$
Rushing	730	$(751 + 775 + 621 + 771) \div 4 = 729.5$
Allowed	727.5	$(721 + 846 + 704 + 639) \div 4 = 727.5$
Passing	730	$(766 + 704 + 664 + 787) \div 4 = 730$
Allowed	733	$(780 + 699 + 694 + 760) \div 4 = 733$

Step 16. Get the ratios again, based on the adjusted totals.

	A	B	C	D	
OER	.92	.88	1.14	1.04	$(.073 + .073 + .086 + .086 + .041) \div 5 \div .069 = 1.04$
DER	.96	.89	1.07	1.06	$(.065 + .065 + .088 + .088 + .058) \div 5 \div .069 = 1.06$
Rushing	.98	.97	1.05	1.01	$(751 + 751 + 775 + 775 + 621) \div 5 \div 730 = 1.01$
Allowed	.97	.94	1.04	1.06	$(721 + 721 + 846 + 846 + 704) \div 5 \div 727.5 = 1.06$
Passing	.99	1.00	1.02	.99	$(766 + 766 + 704 + 704 + 664) \div 5 \div 730 = .99$
Allowed	.98	1.01	1.01	1.00	$(780 + 780 + 699 + 699 + 694) \div 5 \div 733 = 1.00$

Step 17. Get the final adjusted totals based on the level of competition.

	A	B	C	D	
OER	.073	.087	.042	.075	$(.076 \div 1.01 = .075)$
DER	.065	.088	.058	.063	$(.064 \div 1.02 = .063)$
Rushing	751	767	615	771	$(817 \div 1.06 = 771)$
Allowed	736	872	684	614	$(620 \div 1.01 = 614)$
Passing	773	704	664	787	$(787 \div 1.00 = 787)$
Allowed	780	699	694	760	$(752 \div .99 = 760)$

Step 18. Predict rushing and passing yards for A vs. B, and C vs. D.

	A	B	C	D	
Rushing	179	155	103	145	$[(684 \div 727.5) \times (771 \div 5)] = 145)$
Passing	147	149	138	149	$[(694 \div 732.5) \times (787 \div 5)] = 149)$
Total Yards	326	304	241	294	$145 + 149 = 294$

Step 19. Get the average number of turnovers per team, per game.

Total Fumbles Lost = 41 $(10+15+8+8 = 41)$
Total Interceptions = 37 $(12+10+4+11 = 37)$
Total Turnovers = 78 $(37+41 = 78)$
Average Per Game, Per Team 3.9 $(78/4/5 = 3.9)$

Step 20. Predicted turnovers for and against each team.

	A	B	C	D	
For	3.88	3.72	3.76	4.24	$([(15 + 13)/5 + (3.9 \times 4)]/5 = 4.24)$
Against	4.00	4.12	3.60	3.88	$([(8 + 11)/5 + (3.9 \times 4)]/5 = 3.88)$

Step 21. Adjust predicted total yardage for turnovers.

	A	B	C	D	
Final Yardage	335	298	237	299	(4.24 + 3.60 − 3.76 − 3.88) × 50/2 = 5) (294 + 5 = 299)

Step 22. Get the predicted score for each team.

	A	B	C	D	
Predicted OER	.0931	.0819	.0383	.0630	[(.058 ÷ .069) × .075 = .0630]
Predicted Score	31.2	24.4	9.1	18.8	(299 × .0630 = 18.8)

Step 23. Now we adjust for the home-team advantage, and we predict A will beat B 33 to 29, and D will beat C 21 1/2 to 8 1/2 (we predict total points of 51.1 and 26.6, respectively). So we can bet Team A giving 1 point or less, since we predict they will win by 4, and we will bet if our prediction differs by at least 3 points from the bookie's point spread. We could bet Team B plus 7 points, Team D giving 10 points, or Team C getting 16 points.

This procedure, after you get used to it, takes about three hours in the sixth week, and seven hours the last week. You can save time by having a separate worksheet for each team. That way you can just sort out a team's opponents to facilitate the comparisons.

10 | Nevada—the Sports Bettor's Paradise

Right now there is only one place in the United States where you can legally bet sports—Nevada. I have never been to northern Nevada, but Las Vegas is heaven to me. My Las Vegas headquarters is the Hollywood Race and Sports Book, which is located downtown, right across from the Mint Hotel. There are four other sports books within a few blocks: the Fremont, the Union Plaza, the El Cortez and Leroy's.

Since the federal gambling tax was reduced from ten to two percent, and the bookmakers decided to pay the tax for the customers, it is now viable to bet sports in Las Vegas. And betting with legal bookies is beautiful, compared to betting with illegal bookies. No hassle about getting paid, no breaking laws, no confusions or mix-ups about who you bet, how much you bet, or at what price. No phone numbers to keep track of, no pickups or deliveries. You just buy a ticket, which has the amount of your bet, the team you bet on, the odds or point spread, and the date. If you win, you go to the cashier's window and collect. If you lose, you file away the ticket. No credit, so there is no temptation to bet money you don't have. They always pay when you win, and they don't tell you to get lost if you are a consistent winner. In fact, I doubt if they even know whether you are a winner or a loser.

There are also many other sports bookies in town, on the strip and in North Las Vegas. So there is plenty of opportunity to "shop" for better odds or point spreads. And you can bet more money than I have ever wanted to, between all these places.

Each bookie joint looks a little different, but they all work just about the same. The point spread or line is posted for each game, on a blackboard or on sliding panels (in the fancier places). The line is usually in a constant state of flux, and the changes are posted as they occur. Different bookie joints have different criteria for when they change the line, but it usually takes a "limit" bet before they will make an adjustment. And they all have different limits, which also change depending on how well the individual bookie is doing. But you can get down plenty of money, so the limits are no problem.

All the betting rules are posted, including the "proposition" bets, such as teasers and parlays. As I have said before, I don't fool with anything but straight bets. You will find that many of the customers do a lot of "proposition" betting among themselves. Beware of these groups. Quite a few of them have some pretty good sucker bets to offer. Don't take them up on anything, period. Not only is it illegal, it is unprofitable. These guys are professional gamblers, and quite a few of them are real sharpies.

Las Vegas, as you might expect, is full of illegal bookies. Stay away from them. They get more legal heat than in any other city in the country. Illegal bookies are a problem to deal with in general, but the problem is much worse in Vegas.

Dealing with illegal bookies, is, in fact, the one element of sports betting that I hate, so I avoid it like the plague. "Georgie," my baseball bookie from Chapter 1, is the only bookie I have ever met. I always let someone else handle all bookmaking transactions for me whenever possible. I don't do the calling, paying, collecting or anything else, except the picking. Whoever made the connection with the bookie is the only one who has any contact with him. The bookies prefer it that way, and so do I. If I don't know them, and they don't know me, neither one of us can get the other into any trouble. For the most part, this has worked very well. When my go-betweens go on vacation, or work late, or whatever, I miss some betting opportunities occasionally, but it is worth it to avoid the contact.

Not that I don't think bookies are nice people. In all my years of betting, I don't know of a single incident of violence on the part of a bookie. And Georgie is a prince of a human being. But it is illegal to make book. I am not sure if it is illegal to bet, and I don't really want to find out. I do know the anti-gambling laws are unfair, hypocritical, and broken by at least half the population. Betting is something that people do, and the laws are unenforceable and ridiculous. But they are laws, and I am going to obey them by doing all my betting in Vegas from now on. Of course, the fact that illegal bookies currently owe me pretty large sums of money I will probably never see has a lot to do with my decision.

I'm sure that my recent bookie problems are the result of my turning "pro" and betting larger amounts. I never had a problem when the sums of money were smaller. So if you are going to deal with bookies, this is an important consideration. Don't let things get to the point where you are owed large sums of money. A good rule is never bet more that one half of a bookie's limit on one game, and make sure he never owes you more than five times his limit. You are much more likely to get paid at this figure. Most bookies are willing to settle at any time when either party owes more than an agreed-upon amount. And I would always have such an agreement.

If the systems and handicapping advice in this book work out so well for you that you decide to make a career of betting, move to Las Vegas. It's the only reasonable place to live if you are a professional gambler. Even if you are only a Vegas vacationer, check out the bookie joints on your next trip. The characters hanging around those places are straight out of Damon Runyon. And it is fun to make a legal sports bet, for a change.

11 | Gamblers—the Winners and the Losers

Ask almost any gambler why he gambles, and he will tell you he gambles to make money, of course. But the fact is, most gamblers play to lose. I have known at least fifty gamblers well, and I have observed thousands of gamblers at the track and in Las Vegas. Although they don't admit it, with rare exception most gamblers expect to lose, want to lose and, in some cases, even need to lose. The result? Most gamblers lose.

Why? People are complicated, so the reasons are complicated. Religion is a major factor in creating the losing psychology. Most serious losers are people with a strong religious background. They have been taught that gambling is a sin, but are doing it anyway. They have also been taught that you are punished for your sins, so they punish themselves by losing. If, by accident, they happen to win, then they have the additional sin of having gotten something for nothing. This is particularly true of Protestants, who are taught that hard work is the only justifiable means of obtaining wealth. Usually, winning calls for a severe dose of losing.

I once had a Protestant friend, Mike, who illustrates my point. Mike was a hard worker, a bus driver by day and bowling-alley maintenance man by night. He was very motivated to accumulate money, and was willing to work hard to do it. One night, a group was going to the harness races. Mike had a rare night off and decided to come along. He had never seen a race of any kind, and he didn't bring much money with him—maybe ten dollars. He didn't want to bet; he was just coming along out of curiosity and camaraderie.

We arrived at the track about forty-five minutes before the first race. I bought a program and showed Mike how to read the past performances, explained parimutuel betting, the daily double, and in general gave him a quick lesson in betting. I took him to the paddock to look at the horses, then went to make my bet. I asked Mike if he wanted to bet, but he said no, he'd just watch. When I got back to our seats, he still hadn't returned. About one minute before post time, he showed up, a big grin on his face.

"I bet the daily double," he said, holding out the ticket for me to examine, "4 and 6."

He had picked two long shots, neither of which showed much. To my amazement, Number 4 won the first race, paying twenty-six dollars.

"Nothing to this," Mike said casually, an expert already. He then expounded on the merits of his second selection as the daily-double possibilities were announced—4 and 6 would pay almost five hundred dollars.

He watched calmly, almost as if the result were a foregone conclusion, as his second horse trotted home in front. The first bet of his life, and he hit a long-shot double, a horse player's dream. By the end of the night, he was up over nine hundred dollars.

"How long has this been going on?" he wanted to know. I told him if he was smart, he'd put his winnings in the bank. But he was hooked. He took off work the next day and went to Arlington Park and won again. Now, as a Protestant, he was in real trouble. He had sinned by gambling. Worse, he had won. That called for serious reprisals.

Within two weeks, Mike was jobless, penniless and homeless. He went to the track night and day, and bet in a frenzy, wagering large amounts on the longest shots in each race. When he had lost everything, and borrowed to the limits of his credit, he disappeared. I have never seen him again. I hope he got a fresh start somewhere, and has stayed away from gambling. With his Protestant psychology, he doesn't stand a chance.

Many gamblers, for whatever reason, are guilt-laden before they become gamblers. They have an overwhelming need for self-punishment. Gambling, and losing, is a more acceptable form of torture than banging one's head against a wall. In a sense, people in this boat are really taking the easy way out. This affliction seems to affect Catholics and Jews more commonly than Protestants. It is marked by chronic, constant losing.

Alfie, a good Catholic, is a perfect example of a guilt-ridden gambler. Alfie used to work for me. He was constantly asking for advances on his pay, and borrowing small sums of money. I heard through my grapevine that he was losing money betting with other employees on various sports events. But Alfie didn't bother with point spreads or odds. Naturally, the "sharpies" he was betting against would gladly take him on when the odds were against him, but refuse when the odds were with him. Of course, he could only lose.

I decided to help him. The first thing I did for him was let him bet through me at the correct bookie odds. His losses dropped to a fraction of what they had been, so he bet more money. Then, I started advising him which bets he shouldn't make. He actually started winning. I sold him five shares in the baseball pool mentioned in the first chapter, and gave him my best horse system. Now he was winning a fairly substantial amount.

Then the guilt took over. He wrecked his car. Then he had a big fight with his wife, and she left him. But he was still winning. So he sold his five shares for $150 when the value was $200. Then he stopped asking me what the line was so he could make his own bets. Pretty soon, he was asking for advances again. I checked around, and he was betting at the wrong odds again. I called him into my office.

"What's going on, Alfie? Do you hate yourself? Why are you making those dumb bets again?" I asked.

"Ah, it's too much trouble to keep all those odds straight," he answered. I argued, but he was adamant. He was going to lose whether I liked it or not. I bugged him about it off and on, and chastised the people who were taking advantage of him. So he quit his job. If I wouldn't let him lose, he was going to get far away from me. The last I heard from him, he was back with his wife, and enjoying himself, losing regularly. He was an extreme case of the guilty gambler, and I guess if I had converted him into a permanent winner, he probably would have killed himself. But it would have been a lot better if he had learned to like himself enough to enjoy winning.

Another major factor in creating losing gamblers is some people's need for anxiety. Gambling to win, having the odds in your favor, does not produce much tension—just a comfortable sense of anticipation. Gambling to lose, on the other hand, can make you a nervous wreck. Many people require a great deal of tension in their lives. Usually they became accustomed to it in childhood. So many parents are like time bombs—ready to blow up any second—that their kids live in a state of constant anxiety, never knowing when their parents' wrath is about to descend upon them. This state becomes "normal." However, when they become adults, the cause of anxiety is removed, and they don't feel "normal" because they aren't anxious. The solution? Gamble, and do it badly, so the sense of impending disaster is present, as it has been all their lives. (Buddy Hackett tells the story of his having gone into the army, where the food is very bland. He had been raised on heavy, spicy Jewish cooking, and he never felt right after the army meals. He decided he was ill, so he went to the camp doctor. The doctor told him his problem was that he wasn't getting indigestion any more. To him, indigestion was normal, and he didn't feel right without it. So it is with people raised on anxiety. They miss it when it isn't there.)

I'll use myself as a former example of a gambler who just wanted to worry, not to win. Once I got into computer programming, my life became very smooth in every respect. The result? No anxiety. I almost didn't know who I was, since my entire life had been one anxious moment after another. My solution? Bet a lot of football games. By then I had developed some winning techniques, and each week I would make my system selections on Wednesday or Thursday, and sit back and wait for the weekend. But on Friday I'd take another look at the schedule, and talk myself into a few more bets. On Saturday morning, I would discover that I had missed even more good bets. By noon, I would have bet thirty games, even though my system had only picked eight or nine. On Sunday morning, usually in an effort to make up my Saturday losses, I would find a reason to bet every single pro game. Then I would nervously pace the floor all day, listening and watching as my money went down the tube. It got so bad, I once spent the whole game rooting for the wrong team. I had forgotten who I had bet, I had so many bets! By Sunday night, I would be exhausted, but not too exhausted to start worrying about next week's games.

Eventually I became a manager of data processing, started to fight with my wife, and didn't need any extra anxiety. I had plenty, so I could concentrate on being a winning gambler. I am now aware of this strange quirk in my personality, and take great pains to make sure I am betting to win, not just to have an excuse to be a "nervous Nellie." This self-awareness is just as important to my success as a gambler as the techniques I use.

The "dreamers" are another group of compulsive losers. They fantasize winning a fortune, and living happily ever after. They are the "plungers," the all-or-nothing players. They don't want to win a little, they tell you, they "want to make a real killing." (This phrase is common among the dreamers.) You know what they are trying to kill? Their dream. They don't want it to come true, because they know the dream is better than the reality. Everything in their life is geared toward "next year." I am convinced they are scared to death that "next year" might come, and then they'll have to live today, right now, and they've never had to do that. They would lose purpose. How many people do you know who have talked most of their lives of retiring, so they could relax and enjoy themselves. Funny that so many of them die either before or—because they've put it off so long—shortly after they retire?

The dreamer needs his dream. Money will make him happy, his dream says. But he has to do something about it, or he won't be able to keep dreaming. Since he can't risk the dream becoming reality, he gambles. If he wins, he gambles more. If he keeps winning, he keeps betting more. Sooner or later, he will lose. Then he can say, "I almost did it," to himself (and everyone else who will listen). "Next time I'll get 'em!"

There is an old guy, named Howie, who hangs around the bookie joints in Las Vegas. Howie is a dreamer. All he talks about is getting lucky enough to win ten grand, the sum he claims will get him out of Vegas and to Florida, where he can be near his kids.

Every two weeks, Howie gets his pension check, pays all his bills, stocks his refrigerator, and heads for the bookie joint —where he proceeds to bet all his money on whatever sport is going at the time. He plays three-, four-, and even five-team parlays, round robins, and generally throws his money away. Well, one Friday he won every baseball game he bet, for a profit of five thousand dollars. Was he happy? No way. He moaned and groaned about how tough it was to make anything in sports betting. "I win every game, and I'm still five thousand dollars short," he complained to anyone who would listen. The next day, with a little encouragement from his cronies, who were sick of hearing him bemoan his meager five-thousand-dollar killing, he bet the whole five thousand on the game of the week on TV. He took the underdog, at odds of 3 to 2 (I think it was San Francisco against Cincinnati). He was delirious when Frisco jumped out to a big lead. But a strange thing happened. As the game went on, and it became clearer that he was going to win, that his dream really would come true, Howie got quieter. When the last out was made, his buddies all came over to congratulate him, but Howie was white-faced, shaken. He sat for an hour before he walked slowly to the cashier and collected his money. While he was counting it, a big smile spread across his face. "I'm in a hot streak," he announced to no one in particular. "I'm gonna take this no-good town for every cent they got." He marched out the door and headed straight for the Mint casino.

He was back in two hours, broke. Relief was written all over his face. He had averted disaster, and avoided his "dream come true." He was just good old tough-luck Howie again, safe in Vegas, where he really wanted to be, living in tomorrow. Tomorrow will never come for Howie, but look at all the todays he's missing.

Finally, many people lose money gambling because they aren't gambling for money. They are gambling for ego satisfaction, or because of an emotional involvement with a team, or because they want revenge. They are what I call "personal" gamblers. Their self-esteem is what they are betting to win, not money. Their gambling is purely emotional, with little or no rationality, so they are easy marks. I think these people really would like to win, but their emotions ruin their chances.

Betting with your heart is fine, if you bet insignificant sums. But too often the heart bettor is goaded into betting big money with little chance of winning, since he is basically trying to buy something money can't buy.

All of you reading this book have known people who gamble to lose. You could probably tell story after story about bizarre gambling situations. If you think about the gamblers you know, the vast majority are guilt-ridden self-punishers, or anxiety seekers, or dreamers, or heart bettors, or some combination of these characteristics. And they are losers.

Most people (women in particular) hate losing. So they

don't gamble. Since most people who do gamble play to lose, the logical conclusion would seem to be, don't gamble. Right? Wrong. My conclusion is, don't gamble unless you are gambling to win. I hope this book has shown you that gambling and winning is possible, and fun.

If gambling turns you on, do it. But do it right. In this book you have been introduced to some winning techniques, and I will illustrate some approaches to developing winning techniques in the following chapters. I will also give you guidelines to recognize losing behavior. I will introduce you to techniques aimed at devloping a winning psychology. But first, before you decide every gambler is a loser, let me tell you about some of the winners I know.

Herschel is a professional gambler. He has never been employed. His apartment is in a friend's name, he does not have a driver's license, or credit cards, and even uses a pseudonym when he makes a reservation at a restaurant. He selected his name for the purposes of this book, and I had to agree to keep his description out of the book before he would permit me to use any "Herschel" stories.

He is not, however, anonymous to the bookmaking community. He is well known, though not well loved. He has broken more than one bookie. I do not know his income, but he is not cheap, and hops around the country as often as most of us go to a supermarket. His games are poker, football, baseball, and basketball.

Herschel is a student of these games, and understands them well. But his real edge is an intuitive understanding of human psychology, particularly the psychology of gamblers. For this reason, he is a deadly poker player. He also fares well at football and basketball, very emotional games. Baseball is the one area where he flounders, though he benefits there from having access to my selections. But head-to-head poker is his real game. He is almost unbeatable for one reason: If he doesn't think he will win, he doesn't play. But if he thinks he can psyche out his opponent, watch out.

Herschel understands his own potential for the losing psychology. If he starts losing, he says, "I must hate myself these days." And then he punishes himself. He won't smoke cigars until he starts winning. Or he will just stop betting for a few days. Once, when he felt he had played poker stupidly, he walked home from the game in a driving snowstorm. This is only remarkable because it was a thirty-mile walk. An occasional motorist would stop and offer him a lift. But he refused, because, "If I must punish myself, this is much cheaper than doing it at the gaming tables." It works for him. He keeps the devil (guilt) from his doorstep well enough to make a living by gambling. The bread he eats is earned in the arena of games. Herschel has structured things so he needs to win, wants to win, and does win.

Georgie, my colorless bookie, is another winner. I can hear you saying, "Of course he wins. He's a bookie." But most bookies go broke, for two reasons. First, most of them gamble on their own and have the same likelihood of being losers as any gambler. Second, in one sense, the odds are stacked against them. The process of selection eliminates losers as they run out of money, and the winners are the survivors, whose capital grows. Sooner or later, the winners get most bookies, primarily because most bookies don't believe you can win through skill. They decide the winners have been lucky, and will lose sooner or later, so they keep booking their bets. And keep losing to them, until they are wiped out.

Georgie, on the other hand, is in it to win. He doesn't gamble on his own. He is not a handicapper, and has no interest in the sports he books. He never even listens to a game on the radio, which is why he mispronounces so many of the names. But he understands his business perfectly. He is delighted to find a winning customer. He doesn't fight them, he joins them, piggybacking on their action. Frequently, because he is a bookie, he bets at better odds than his winning customer is getting. As a big-money bookie, Georgie has access to other big-money bookies. Normally, he tries to juggle things so that he has exactly the same amount bet on both teams in a sports event. For example, say the Bears are a 6 1/2 point favorite over the Giants, and Georgie's customers bet $5,000 on the Bears, but only $3,000 on the Giants (laying 11–10, of course). Georgie will try to "lay off" (bet with another bookie) the excess $2000 bet on the Bears, leaving him in a situation where he is certain to win the "vigorish" (the bookie's percentage, in this case 11–10 when it should be an even bet), or $300. (No matter which team wins, the winners get $3,000, the losers blow $3300. Of course, the line frequently changes, and this ideal situation cannot always be arranged.) When Georgie has a winning customer, like me, he will keep imbalances in the direction of the winner's bet. In the above example, if his winning customer had bet the Giants, he would keep the action instead of laying it off. So he would then have a bet on the Giants plus 6 points, but he would be getting 11–10 instead of giving odds of 11–10. This is a significant difference. Let's say the winning customer bets a thousand a game, winning 60, losing 40. His profit is 60,000 minus 44,000, or $16,000. If Georgie made the same bets, getting 11–10, his profit would be 66,000 minus 40,000, or $26,000. You can see why he loves finding a winner.

Georgie's search for winning bettors led to my association with him. I had bet horses and football through Herschel for several years, winning consistently. As we got to know each other, he discovered that baseball was my first love, though I had never bet baseball, because the minimum bet in Chicago was so high. (One of my cardinal rules is to never bet more than I can comfortably afford to lose). I frequently complained to Herschel about not being able to bet baseball, because I was sure I could win. Herschel thought of Georgie. He went to him and explained my winning history, and asked Georgie to take my action, just to see if I was a winner. My original $100 bets were far below Georgie's minimum, but he made the time investment anyway. As I've already described, it worked out to our mutual benefit. Georgie even paid me a commission to make sure I kept betting with him after I had moved up to betting amounts that provided me access to other bookies.

Georgie's edge is his lack of ego involvement. He doesn't have to be the brains behind the action. He is perfectly happy to merely accept money as his payoff. This is virtually unheard of among gamblers. Georgie has turned his edge into a gold mine. I can only guess, but he must make a quarter of a million a year, in a business where most of the competition goes broke.

This book is not really aimed at big-time bookies or professional gamblers, though it could help them too. It is really aimed at people who want to enjoy the thrill of betting and make a profit while they are at it.

Jim D. is such a gambler. He probably averages between one and three thousand dollars a year in gambling profits. Jim, like I did, worked with computers for a living. When I met him, he had literally never made a bet in his life. I introduced him to horse racing, taking him to the track. He gave me a dollar a race to add to my bets, which he insisted I explain to him in detail. So I handicapped each race out loud, explaining the rationale behind each selection. We won, and he was intrigued by the racing form in the same way I had been. He was also fascinated by the people at the track, the excitement of the crowd, and most of all, loved cheering home the winners. His interest made me a little nervous, in view of what had happened to Mike, the only other Protestant I had introduced to gambling.

But Jim was a different story. The next day, he went to the library to get a book on horse racing, only to discover they did not stock gambling books. So he went out and purchased every book available on the subject of horse racing. Within a week he had read them all. Then he began buying the racing form every day, trying out the theories expounded in the books, but on paper only. He then reread the best of the books, Tom Ainslie's *The Compleat Horse Player,* an excellent primer in handicapping. (Since then, Mr. Ainslie has improved on this with his *Encyclopedia of Horse Racing,* far and away the best book on the subject of horse racing.)

By the time Jim made his first wager, he was well versed in the art of handicapping. No expert, but certainly not the rank amateur most of us horse players were when we started.

Not long after his introduction to the horses, a group of us started a regular poker game. Jim was terrible the first night, as you might expect of someone who wasn't even sure if a flush beat a straight. By the next time we played, he had read two books on playing poker. He was no longer a complete fish, and within a few weeks he was winning regularly. It was an amazing approach for a beginner, learning how to gamble from books.

Jim's life had taken on new dimensions. Every Wednesday, poker; every Saturday, the track. And he loved them both. I assumed he would become a true gambler, with the normal losing attitudes. But it never happened. He liked horse racing, poker, *and* winning. They made ideal hobbies. That was twelve years ago. His gambling has increased only to the extent of a yearly trip to Las Vegas. Of course, he read a book on blackjack, and wins at blackjack too. He still plays poker every Wednesday, in what must be one of the most durable continuous friendly games going. I have long since dropped out, because I'm a bad poker player (and finally admitted it to myself). He still goes to the track every Saturday the horses are in Chicago. He has gone from a $2 bettor to a $10 bettor, but he's never made a bet over $10. I have never seen him plunge in an effort to get even. I have never heard him dream of making a killing.

Jim gambles for fun. He makes a little money at it, which makes it more fun. I estimate there are millions of Americans who could improve the quality of their lives by adopting Jim's approach to gambling. He picked games he likes, learned how to win through study and experience, and maintained a sensible, self-fulfilling attitude. It is possible that, in the real sense of winning, Jim profits more from gambling than either Herschel or Georgie. Jim plays for the right stakes. Pleasure. It seems simple, but it is a rare thing, unfortunately.

Larry, my telephone friend from the first chapter, may be the most successful gambler I know, if you measure success by the amount of pleasure obtained. He bets on poker, gin rummy, baseball, football, basketball, and his own bowling. He is an outstanding gin player, deadly at poker, knows sports inside out, averages around 140 at bowling, and remembers more details about these things than seems possible. He also, incidentally, has a Ph.D. in mathematics. All this is remarkable in itself, but even more remarkable when you consider the fact that he has been totally blind since he was two years old.

I played poker with him once. We played with braille-coded cards. The dealer was required to announce each card as it was dealt. In every other respect, it was a normal poker game. Larry did not require being told anyone's up cards; he memorized them as they were dealt. Needless to say, he knew every card which had been folded, the precise betting from the beginning of each hand, and probably from the first hand of the night on. But the amazing thing about playing poker with Larry is his total enjoyment of the game. He was like a child with a new toy on Christmas morning. He was happy when he folded correctly, when he guessed right about the winner of hands he didn't play, but mostly, when he won a hand he was in heaven. His joy was indescribable, and he knew exactly how much was in each pot without counting it.

I have never known anyone who wanted to win more than Larry does, or enjoyed it more. He relishes the entire gambling process—deciding which bets to make, the drama of the event, and most of all, the thrill of victory. I love to watch a game with Larry, he on his end of the phone, both of us listening to our transoceanics, both of us predicting what will happen next, admiring the great players, bemoaning the mindless strategies of most managers, cheering the key plays, sharing the winning experience.

Although I know he has never seen a game with his eyes, he knows more about the rudiments than most fans. He watches the games with his ears, picking up on every detail, totally aware of what is taking place. I asked Larry what "pictures" he has in his mind when he watches a game. He says it is a totally abstract concept. He has no mental image of what he is hearing. What happens simply *is.*

When Larry gambles, he wins so many things. Money, of course, plus the pleasure of participation in the event, even as a spectator, and the ego satisfaction of being a winner. But most of all, he loves each win. He is a tireless winner.

Larry is not rich from his gambling because he can't tolerate anxiety, so he can only bet small amounts. He would prefer to win less money, and not spoil his fun. He protects his pleasure by understanding what gambling is all about, having fun.

Larry's edge in gambling, aside from his tremendous intelligence, is his *desire* to win. No guilty throwaway bets for him; though he realizes he can't win every bet (I think), he absolutely wants to. With that kind of purposefulness, he can't help but win.

Each of these people has his own approach to winning, and their approaches are all different from mine. But we all have one thing in common: we want to win and are willing to work at it. None of us is perfect—we all have lapses and weaknesses—but each of us gains from gambling. We are participants, vital, involved, and face each new day with the expectation that something good will probably happen to us. We will win. Our lives are fuller, enriched by the winning experience. I hope this book helps you get as much out of gambling as Herschel, Georgie, Jim D., Larry, and myself.

12 | What are Your Personal Best Gambling Opportunities?

Before we talk about gambling opportunities, let's define gambling. To me, most of life is a gamble. You gamble when you buy a used car, take a girl out to dinner, change jobs, get married, put your money in a bank, don't take your umbrella, buy life insurance.

But this book is about gambling money. To most of the world, any risk where you can lose your whole investment—like betting a ball game—is a gamble. Whereas a more limited risk, like buying a stock, where you probably won't lose everything, is an investment. To me, they are both gambles. My definition of gambling is the investment of money where you have the possibility of gaining or losing money and the *purpose* of the investment is to gain money. By this definition, buying a used car is not a gamble. Buying a plot of land as an investment is a gamble.

What will you do with the part of your income that isn't necessary for your everyday existence? You can gamble by putting it in a bank and hope the inflation rate doesn't exceed the interest rate by too much. This is a gamble with virtually no chance of winning. It is far and away the most common bet made. It is also a pretty bad bet. Almost anyone, with a little hard work, can come up with a better gamble than that.

Anyone with excess money has the opportunity to use that money to make more money by gambling on something that has favorable odds. Choosing the best gambling opportunity and learning how to capitalize on that opportunity is a different proposition for each person. In order to make these decisions, each person must ask himself several questions.

1. What gambling opportunities are available to you?
There are basically four kinds of gambles a person can take with his money. He can bet against an institution—like a bookie, race track, or casino. He can bet against another person, or persons—as in bridge, poker, golf, or pool. He can bet on the increase in value of something tangible, like a company, a piece of land, an antique, or a cow. Or, he can bet on the stability or decline of the economy, by buying bonds and bank certificates.

Anyone can bet on the economy. The odds you get depend on how much you have to invest and how long you are willing to invest it for. Historically, this is a cinch loser.

Anyone can bet on tangibles. The odds here depend on what you buy and how you buy it. If you are smart, you can have very favorable odds. If you have a lot of money to risk, you can get even more favorable odds. The better "games" for gambling on tangibles are: the stock market, real estate, the commodities market, foreign currency, gold and other precious metals, collector's items and private enterprises. These are clearly excellent gambling opportunities because so many people have done well with them. The fact that they are superior to the gamble of banking your money is obvious when you consider that the banks take that money and gamble heavily in tangibles. The major drawback to this kind of gambling is that it requires a fairly substantial sum of money and is generally a long-term gamble, though not always. Some dramatic things can happen to the value of tangibles. You cannot, however, ordinarily expect to increase your total capital by more than 20 percent a year, unless you are exceptionally skillful.

Head-to-head gambling is available to everyone, at least on a small scale. You can always find someone to bet with on something. The availability of large-scale head-to-head gambling will depend on where you live. In Las Vegas, people play golf for as much as five thousand dollars a hole. There are private poker games where you need ten thousand dollars to sit down. Most big cities have an abundance of big-money card games. Depending on the circles you travel in, you can find people willing to bet almost any amount on anything. Backgammon, bridge, poker, gin rummy, pool, golf, bowling, pinochle, spectator sports, the list is almost endless.

If you don't have enough money to make gambling on tangibles a huge profit maker, head-to-head gambling is the best possible way to make a lot of money. If you can develop a superior ability at any head-to-head game, there are people who will let you take substantial sums of money from them. I know more people who make big money gambling head to head than from any other form of gambling. The beauty of this form of gambling is that you can pick your competition. You never have to play a superior opponent twice.

The biggest disadvantage of head-to-head gambling is that you must beat another human being out of his money face to face. This can be physically dangerous. But more important, it can make you feel guilty, and that is the worst thing that can happen to a gambler. I can't gamble head to head. I can't stand to see the other person's pain.

All the gambling in this book involves betting against an institution. Here is where availability becomes a big problem. Not everyone lives in Las Vegas, so they can't play casino games regularly or bet with legal bookies. Not everyone is willing to bet with illegal bookies and many people don't have access to them. If you live near a race track, harness-race track, dog track, or Jai Alai fronton, you have those betting opportunities. Institutional gambling has the disadvantage of being heavily taxed or having a large built-in edge in favor of the "house." It has the advantage of being well financed, so it is possible to win large sums of money without denting the "house's" bankroll. It also provides a large turnover because of the number of betting transactions available. If you are good, you can double your capital annually.

2. *What are your talents?* Different kinds of gambling require different talents. If you are a good golfer, bowler, or tennis player, you can make lots of money, especially if you are a good hustler. When I was quite young, I made enough money from bowling to support myself for four years. You don't have to be the best in the world, just know your level of ability and be a good judge of other people's ability. Then all you have to do is find people not as good as you to compete with. It can be an excellent source of income.

Good card sense is a tremendous talent that is easily capitalized on. It helps most in games like hearts, gin rummy, pinochle and whist. There is plenty of money flying around on those games.

Being able to "read" people can make you a great poker player or liar's poker player. Being good at games, like chess or backgammon, can be converted into hard cash.

Having a lot of friends in the right places can really help in playing the "tangibles" games, like the stock market or real estate.

Computer knowledge can be applied to a vast number of gambling situations, as can statistical skill, math aptitude, or just high intelligence in general. Specific kinds of knowledge can be converted to a gambling edge, particularly knowledge of sports and economics.

Political connections can give you the edge in many kinds of "investments."

What each person should do is take an inventory of his skills and weaknesses. The search for the proper gambling opportunity starts with matching your talents with the available opportunities.

3. What do you enjoy? Whatever you do, you increase your real profit if you enjoy it. Even if you don't make a killing, if you have fun trying, you are ahead of the game. It is extremely dangerous to gamble on something that is boring, or tedious, or just plain not fun. Too many people make sure they lose just to get it over with.

If you enjoy sports participation, that's a good thing to bet on. If the Dow Jones averages and *Fortune* magazine turn you on, play the market. If you love cards, you have plenty of games to turn to. If you like solving complicated problems, try the horses. If you like dealing with people, go into business. If you match what you like with what you are good at, then look for the right opportunity to tackle using the combination, and you are well on your way to being a winner.

4. What stakes can you afford to play for? If you only have a few hundred bucks a year to play with, don't tackle the stock market or real estate or any game where a huge bankroll gives you a big edge. You need a situation where you can expect a large number of transactions, with a small per-transaction investment, like poker or head-to-head sports, or the horses. You can bet football with an investment of $200 or more. But for baseball, unless you find some partners, you'll need more in order to cover the minimum bet with most illegal bookies. In Las Vegas, you can bet $10 a game, so a bankroll of $300 to $400 is enough.

If you can afford to gamble several thousand a year, the reasonably high turnover games are more attractive, like baseball, tournament bowling, or the commodity market.

If you can afford tens of thousands, then the big money games are best—the stock market, gold, real estate, or high-stakes poker. There is little point in tackling the limited wager markets, like horse racing, unless you have access to unusually high limit bookies. I would say once your goals exceed earnings of $100,000 a year, sports betting no longer fills the bill.

If you are not in the right financial position for the gambling opportunity you choose, you stand much less chance of winning. The small bettor playing the big bettor's game *always* loses. The big bettor playing for peanuts rarely cares enough to win.

5. Finally, do you have the right temperament for the gambling opportunity? This is critical. If you are impatient and like a lot of action, don't touch the long-range gambles like the stock market. You will trade yourself into a frazzle. These games require patience. If you get nervous under pressure, don't gamble head to head. I took a lot of money from superior bowlers because they folded in the clutch. If you suffer from anxiety or can't stand tension, don't bet on sports or horses; they will drive you crazy.

If you are really tightfisted and don't want to risk a penny, put your money in the bank. You can fool yourself into thinking you aren't losing. But, ten years from now, just try to buy what you could have bought with that money today.

Face it, folks, life *is* a gamble. Like it or not, you either spend your money or bet with it. There ain't no other choice.

How did I pick my gambling opportunities? At first, I just fell into betting horses and bowling by accident. After that, it was a very similar process to the one outlined above, although a reassessment of my talents, likes, and temperament, as well as changes in my finances, have made radical changes in my selections.

In terms of opportunity, Chicago has almost everything, from horses to sports to the commodity market. It doesn't have casinos, but it does have junkets to Las Vegas. The opportunities for head-to-head gambling are countless. So I had my pick of opportunities.

The horses were a good first choice for me because I love solving complicated problems; I had a lot of the skills needed to beat the sport; I like a lot of action, and I didn't have much money, so I needed a high turnover situation. I tried gin rummy back when I didn't have much money, but I was terrible. I liked it; there were plenty of people around to play; it fit my finances and personality, but my talents didn't match the game's requirements, so I gave it up.

Bowling was great because I had the talent to carry a 200+ average; I loved it; there were plenty of tournaments and pot games, and it required very little investment, with a fair payoff.

I tried the harness races too, because it had all the same characteristics as horse racing, but I never enjoyed watching the races as much and, back in those days, bookies wouldn't touch the harness races. Besides which, I always lost, so I gave up the harness races.

As I got older and a little more affluent, sports betting became more realistic because my finances allowed me to bet more per transaction. At this point, bowling became less attractive because the time investment versus the dollar return got to be less than I could make working. Besides, I had lost my enthusiasm for the game.

Baseball was the perfect fit when I finally got together enough money to afford it, though I jumped the gun a little by taking on shareholders. Basketball is my current major project, so I will have sports action the year round.

College football and college basketball are good opportunities for me, except I don't really enjoy the games enough to spend the time keeping track of so many teams. I have tried them both and failed, due at least partially to a lack of interest. They may just be too hard for me to beat.

Sports betting is currently my sole source of income. It is profitable enough so that I was able to give up a $55,000-a-year income as a computer consultant. But I am finding that it, too, has its limitations. It will never make me a millionaire.

So I am ready for the biggest form of gambling, the "tangibles" games. I have carefully analyzed each "tangibles" game, matching opportunities with my personality, preferences, skills, and financial situation.

I rejected the stock market because I don't think you can beat the insiders' information edge and don't see any good way to approach the problem. The computer won't help; I've tried it already. You can't anticipate or predict what the big guys, banks and mutual funds, are going to do, or what earth-shaking events will send the market zooming up or down.

Real estate is a great opportunity, but I don't have quite enough money or patience for that game yet. Maybe later. I am learning a little about it because it may become feasible in the near future, but for now it is still over my head, financially.

The commodities market is very attractive. It offers the potential for large gains in a short time. I have a friend who has made millions in commodities. He assures me I have the right kind of mind for it, and he is willing to buy me a seat on any exchange that I choose and teach me the ropes. But I don't like the game. I find it dull and lonely. (A problem with sports betting—it is a very lonely life. After years of managing people, talking for a living, it is very hard to spend most of your life in silence.)

After examining all the possible "tangibles" I could gamble on, I decided to gamble on myself and become an entrepreneur. Working for other people is something I hope to never do again. Gambling for a living is too lonely and has too low an upper limit to suit me. That leaves going into business for myself. The two things I know most about are computers and gambling. I enjoy solving problems, talking to people, teaching, organizing things, travel and gambling. I am a born know-it-all and could talk about sports, gambling, and Las Vegas all day if anyone wants to listen. And I love action. The question is, how to put all those things together.

The answer I have come up with is to start a gambling school, using the computer in as many ways as possible. Since I love Chicago and Las Vegas, the school has to allow me to travel back and forth between the two. In addition, new gambling techniques are fascinating and the school should make it easy to find people with new and interesting ideas.

Some of the products that can be offered are:

1. Introductory courses in casino gambling, including an explanation of the procedures, etiquette, and rules to all

casino games. Combine this with the fundamentals of good gambling and people going to a casino for the first time will have more fun and a much better chance of making money.

2. Advanced courses in horse racing, baseball, football, blackjack, taught by me, and courses in other forms of gambling taught by friends of mine who are experts in those games.

3. Guided tours to Las Vegas, helping people with their gambling, showing them the better places to gamble, eat, drink, making dinner and show reservations, using connections to arrange freebies for the bigger bettors; and, in general, helping people have a better time in Vegas.

4. Teaching people to use the computer to help their gambling and providing computer time to develop winning techniques.

5. Provide the kind of betting information I use for betting baseball, football, horses, basketball, et cetera. Doing the hard work for people and giving them the information edge that can make them winners.

6. Provide learning aids for those gambling situations where there is a lot of memorization involved, such as recordings of my blackjack system.

7. Finally, get enough gamblers together to provide a voting bloc of sufficient size to combat the punitive antigambling legislation that makes profitable gambling more and more difficult.

I know I can teach gambling because I have been doing it successfully for years. I don't think there is a gambler in the world I couldn't teach something. By the same token, there are plenty of people I can learn from. My customers will get their money's worth. If the venture succeeds, I'll make more than I could by hording my secrets and I'll learn more winning techniques in the process. Like any gamble, it might not work out, but the odds seem favorable. The products are worth more than the cost, there is little or no competition, and gambling is increasing in popularity by leaps and bounds. The only question is my ability as a businessman. I have spent my whole life giving things away. That's no way to run a business. But I can promise to give every customer more than his money's worth. I hope that is the way to run a business. Wish me luck.

13 | Developing a Winning Approach

Once you have selected a gambling opportunity, you must develop a winning approach. Hopefully, you will have selected sports betting, and a lot of your work is done for you already. Even if you take a shot at sports betting, the day will come when you will tackle a new opportunity.

The first step is to learn the rules completely. Find out if the rules vary (like from bookie to bookie, or casino to casino). If they do, make sure you take advantage of the best set of rules for you. Shop around until you are satisfied you are getting the best deal available.

Next, you must know exactly what the odds are on a random bet winning. This establishes the degree of superiority you must reach to be a winner. Don't take on a "tough" percentage unless you have good reason to believe you can beat it.

Evaluate the competition. If at all possible, you want John Q. Public as your competition. The best games are those where the average guy is the man to beat. Avoid taking on professionals if you can. If it is a game where you can select the competition, make sure you have a substantial edge. If the competition is out of your control, make sure you have a pretty good idea what you are up against. Never take on a tough percentage *and* tough competition.

Whatever you do, don't let yourself get into a position where you can be cheated. Don't play cards with strangers, or sports either, without a referee or "host" you trust. If you think a game is dishonest, try something else. If the amount of dishonesty is minimal or open to question, try it very carefully. Developing a winning edge won't do you any good if you can get cheated or stiffed. (I have totally given up illegal bookies for that very reason).

Get hold of every piece of information you can on the subject. Read every book, find out who the acknowledged experts are; if you can get to know one and pick his brain, do it. If you can develop an information edge by keeping records, do it. If you can get access to inside information, do it. The key to overcoming the house percentage and the competition and even dishonesty is information. You must take advantage of all developed expertise. If someone else is keeping a lot of records and publishing them, take advantage of the information. Use every tool at your disposal to increase the number of facts on which you base your gambles.

Next, make sure the "insiders" don't have an insurmountable information advantage. You can be ten times smarter, and work ten times as hard, but if your competition knows twice as much as you, they will beat you to death. You just can't beat a marked deck unless you marked it.

At this point, if you still feel your love of the game, special abilities, and knowledge or potential knowledge are enough to overcome the obstacles, you are ready to analyze the game.

Most games are a matter of skill in execution or skill in prediction. Games of execution require a different approach than games of prediction.

Execution consists of three phases:

1. Knowing correct execution.
2. Practicing correct execution.
3. Using correct execution strategically.

Using blackjack as a model, the first thing you must learn

is what correct execution consists of. You can get this from a book. When I took up bowling, I watched good bowlers, read books by good bowlers, and took lessons from good bowlers. In either case, you must start with an awareness of what is the best way to play the game.

The second step is the perfection of the techniques of correct execution. Practice is the only way to do this. To become a blackjack expert, you must spend hours learning the system and hours practicing the system before you will be able to execute it in the real situation in a casino. Bowling obviously takes practice. I bowled one hundred games a week for a year to become a 195-average bowler. "Practice makes perfect" is not just an old saw.

Finally, you must use your ability to execute strategically. In blackjack, this means hiding the fact that you are a winner successfully enough to be permitted to play. Actual experience and analysis of that experience is the only way. You must continuously react to your opponent's (the casino's) strategy to remain successful. In bowling, the strategy consists of successfully analyzing the lane conditions, and adapting to what is required to score well under the prevailing conditions. Practice got me to 195, but experience and analysis got me to 202. It took three additional years to reach the optimum for my skills because the strategy required eluded me for that long. In any execution game, strategy is the final key to success. You must adapt to changes, understand the strategical requirements, and fit your strategies to your skills in order to succeed. This requires careful observation and analysis of what you experience. If you only go as far as your talent takes you, you cheat yourself out of too much.

The last element in an execution proposition is to select your opposition carefully. I don't play blackjack in the Bahamas because the rules are tougher. I could probably still win, but why bother with those disadvantages when you can get a better deal in Las Vegas? In bowling, I never took on a superior opponent. I preferred bowling a lower average bowler and spotting pins. The higher your average, the more likely you are to bowl your average or above. Your low games are more under average than a lower average bowler's. His high games are more over average than yours. So you figure to beat him with a spot of the difference in averages more often than not. In addition, I had the edge in the clutch because I had more experience bowling for money. You must use your execution skills in the best possible situation to be a winner.

Prediction gambles are a different proposition. These games are a matter of analysis. The first step in the analysis is to determine which "variables," or pieces of information, contribute to the result you are trying to predict. You must identify the facts available to you that have a bearing on the outcome. To do this, you must have a solid understanding of the game you are attempting to predict, because a large number of facts are meaningless (or complicated by the circumstances which cause them). If you were looking at horse racing, you might decide that a horse's name could be a useful fact because so many horses with the word "Bold" in their name seemed to do well, as did horses with the word "Ruler" in their names. Of course, a horse player would know Bold Ruler was a great sire, and these words would only signify something if the name had been selected because Bold Ruler was the sire. But many horses have "Bold" and "Ruler" in their names and are not related to Bold Ruler. It is a farfetched example of poor fact selection, but illustrates what can result from lack of knowledge.

So the first step in conquering a prediction game is to learn how it works so you can identify the predictive variables. That is important, but it is also the easiest part of your task. Deciding how each fact functions is the really hard part. This is where a knowledge of the game becomes even more important. The reason is simple. At this point, you have literally millions of potential approaches to determining how to evaluate and use the facts at your disposal. The computer is almost useless for narrowing down approaches, because a computer only knows what *you* choose to tell it.

This is the reason it has taken so long to get computers to play a decent game of chess. For a good chess player, an enormous number of possible moves on each turn are almost instantly discarded. The good player concentrates his analysis on a small number of potentially good moves, no matter how far ahead he is thinking. Finding ways to get a computer program to discard the completely illogical moves is almost impossible. So, even though it can compute hundreds of thousands times faster than a human, it can't use knowledge to eliminate dozens of possibilities in the few seconds that an experienced, knowledgeable human expert can.

Even if you have a computer at your disposal, you must decide how to tackle a particular gambling situation. If you don't have a computer handy, this decision is even more critical because you can't overcome mistakes as rapidly as a machine.

Therefore, your initial approach must be very carefully thought out and evaluated. There are three basic kinds of approaches:

1. To actually attempt to fit *all* the predictive variables together to come up with the precise odds on all the possible outcomes—the approach I used in my baseball system. This requires an excellent understanding of the game, a minimum of interactive variables, a relatively small number of predictive facts, and a stable structure. If a game fits this general description, you must find the best way to learn how the predictive variables function. The answer could be intuition, research, mathematical or statistical analysis, or some variables could work in a self-evident way. This will never be an easy decision— otherwise, everyone could make it and winning would be easy. It is never easy to win with the total predictive approach.

2. Alternatively, you can attempt to isolate variables that are *more* predictive than the competition believes. This approach is much simpler and is especially effective if the game is complicated, has a large number of inter-

active variables, and has a stable structure. It is the approach I used in developing my horse racing systems. The approach here is always some kind of empirical research, but the methods available are numerous. They range from complex statistical techniques to simply checking past performance for the individual variables. This general type of approach is usually best when you first tackle a given game. You learn a lot and become better able to try one of the other approaches.

3. To just take in the facts, observe results, and let your own computer, your brain, work out the values on its own. This is how most people do it, and it works very well if you have a touch of *genius* where the particular game is concerned. This is so rare I wouldn't count on it. However, if you have gone through the analytical and research processes described above, you don't need to be a genius. If you have a reasonably good idea of what the facts are worth mathematically, you might be able to take it the rest of the way and make accurate predictions intuitively. This is my primary approach to football. I have analyzed the predictive facts, I make sure I study them, but the final decision-making process is largely intuitive. Some games, like the stock market, are so complex you can't beat them any other way (except with inside information).

Before you take on any game using the intuitive approach, evaluate your history as a decision-maker. If you have a good track record in making decisions, you have a chance of being a good intuitive gambler. If your "hunches" turn out to be right most of the time, your subconscious mind is probably very smart. If not, don't take this approach. Ninety-five percent of all the losers I know are intuitive gamblers. Only about half the winners take this approach.

Once you have selected your game and your approach and have developed what you feel is the ability to win, try it out in theory only, or for very small amounts. Chances are you won't do very well at first. Don't despair. You will get better.

Keep thinking and trying new things until you begin winning. When you have reached the point where you think you are a winner, you are ready to develop your money management plan.

Money management can't turn a losing proposition into a winning one. If the odds are against you, they are against you, no matter how you bet. But bad money management can turn a winning proposition into a loser. This is easily demonstrated. Let's say your total bankroll is one thousand dollars. If I came up to you and said you could bet me any amount that the first card I turned in a deck was a spade, and I would give you ten-to-one odds, you would have a tremendous advantage, since one fourth of the cards are spades. If I also said you could make this bet fifty times or until I lost ten thousand dollars, what would you do? Clearly, you could ruin a good thing with poor money management. If you bet the whole thousand on the first card, you could lose everything and the game would be over. The fact that the law of averages or the percentages were on your side would be meaningless if you didn't permit them to operate. By the same token, a ten-dollar bet would be wasting an opportunity to make a lot more money. This betting opportunity would be maximized by intelligent money management. You could turn into a loser three-fourths of the time, win $750 half the time, or ten thousand. Or you could start with forty-dollar wagers and increase your bets as your bankroll increased—winning ten thousand dollars 98 percent of the time, and over seven thousand virtually every time. Money management would make this proposition a practical cinch if it were done the best possible way.

My money management system is based on the following assumption.

1. I will make a 10-percent profit per wager. (You may want to assume a lower percent profit.)
2. I want a fixed sum per wager as spendable money.
3. I have a bankroll that is untouchable. I can't spend it.
4. I can, with reasonable accuracy, predict the percentage of wagers I will win.

This formula is the result of an extensive computer analysis of one year's worth of bets. It minimizes the risk of total loss and maximizes the probability of profit while preserving a high profit, though not the maximum, when things go just right. In the year studied, there were thirty-seven different bankrolls being managed. (I bankroll every kind of bet separately, even on the same situation. For example, my baseball system has a bankroll, and my baseball handicapping has a bankroll.) The computer's job was to select the formula that made me the most money without bankrupting any of the bankrolls associated with a winning proposition. Of the thirty-seven, fourteen would have lost money on a flat bet basis. Three made in excess of 50-percent profits on flat bets. All three produced less profit than they would have using more risky money management formulas, but the overall result would have been *much* worse with the risky formulas.

Here are the elements of the formula:
1. The percentage of winning bets.
2. The number of bets, approximately, per year.
3. The size of my bankroll, or
4. The amount of money I wish to earn, per wager.

You can use the formula to tell you the size of your bankroll or the amount you will earn per wager, depending on your situation. If you have a fixed amount to invest, you must determine the bankroll size. If you are in a position to handle any bankroll, then choose the amount you wish to earn. Most people are limited by bankroll size. When I need investors, I use the amount earned per wager to tell me how much I have to raise.

The formula does not apply to blackjack, dice, or any "tangible" investment. It is useful only for predictive games such as horse racing or baseball. For blackjack or any card game, the maximum bet should be about one percent of your total bankroll. In other words, if you were playing poker, you should have one hundred times the maximum you will have to bet in any one round of betting.

I have never tackled the money management problem for

the "tangibles" games, so I won't guess for you. For me, I would never risk more than half my bankroll on any one venture or purchase. But I am a conservative, and it may be that you can get away with putting all your money into one venture. I wouldn't do it myself.

To illustrate the formula, baseball represents one extreme and a long-shot horse system the other, so let's apply it to both. The first thing we want to do is establish the bankroll size, or per bet return, whichever is the unknown.

For baseball, let's say I decide to make fifty dollars a game. I know from past experience I bet around five hundred games a season and win over 55 percent of all bets. To determine my bankroll size, I perform the following calculations:

1. Multiply 500 games by 50 dollars, giving $25,000, the total amount I wish to win per year, as spendable income.

2. Multiply 55 percent wins by 5 percent (a constant in the formula, determined by the computer) giving the percentage of the bankroll that you may wager per game, or 2.75 percent of your bankroll.

3. Divide 500, the number of bets, by 4 to get the number of bets per betting period: 125. I divide the year into four parts and take four "paydays" a year.

4. Multiply 2.75 times 125 times 10 percent, giving .34, the percentage of profit on your bankroll per period. (The percentage of your bankroll, times the number of bets per period, times the profit per bet.)

5. Pay yourself half the profit each period. Half of .34 is .17.

6. For the second period you will have a bankroll 1.17 times what you started with, so your profit will be .34 times 1.17 or 40 percent profit. Pay yourself half of this profit, or 20 percent. You have now collected 37 percent of your bankroll in profits and retain 1.37 percent of your bankroll for the third betting period.

7. Repeat step 6 for the third period. 1.4 (rounding up from 1.37) times .34 gives a 48-percent profit; you take 23

percent for a total of 60 percent of your original bankroll that you have collected. You have 1.6 times your original bankroll to bet in the last period.

8. 1.6 times .34 is .54, the last-period profit, and you pay yourself all of it. Now you have collected 114 percent of your original bankroll for the year's wagering. You can also now collect the 60 percent you used to bet during the fourth betting period, so your total collection has been 174 percent of the original bankroll.

9. We wanted a total profit of $25,000, so the bankroll is $25,000 divided by 1.74, or 14,368.

10. The bet size is .0275 of the bankroll, or 14367 times .0275, which is $395. I would round these figures to a bankroll of $15,000 and a bet size of $400.

11. After each 125 bets, you take half the profits from that period and recompute the amount you bet per game by multiplying the remaining bankroll by .0275.

For our horse racing example, let's use a system that gets 400 bets a year, with a win percentage of 20 percent and a bankroll of $2,000. Here are the steps to determine how much we will make in a year and per bet.

1. To get the amount of our initial bet per race, multiply 5 percent (the constant) by 20 percent giving one percent, times $2,000, or $20 per race.

2. We will make 100 bets per period, so our first period profit is 100 times $20 times 10 percent, giving $200. We take $100 in profit.

3. The second period, we will bet $21 a race and make $210. We take $105 in profit.

4. The third period we bet $22 a race and win $220. We get $110.

5. The last period, we bet $23 a race and win $230. Our total profits are $860 or a $2.30 profit per race.

The important features of this money management technique are:

1. You must have a "real" bankroll which you do not need for any other purpose. There will be times when even

the best techniques will have you down to less than half your bankroll.

2. You must give yourself each payday and not reinvest until the end of a year. If you always reinvest, losing streaks become even more painful.

3. You cannot recalculate your bet amount more often than four times a year. Too frequent bet fluctuations also exaggerate the effects of losing streaks.

4. If you use the same bankroll for multiple techniques, each additional technique requires a 10 percent increase in your "real" bankroll. For example, I might have as many as fifteen unique horse racing techniques going at once and a total horse racing bankroll of $24,000. My bankroll size per technique is $10,000. If you share bankrolls among techniques, no technique must ever exceed the bet size allowed for your total "real" bankroll.

5. Remember that no system will perform exactly as predicted. But you must follow the rules anyway. You may not make a profit every quarter, or you may make much more than predicted. In either case, you follow the system, or quit betting.

Money management is the most important ingredient in successful gambling. It won't make a winner out of a losing technique, but poor money management will turn even the most powerful winning technique into a loss of money. I know, because I have done it to myself many times. The worst thing you can do is increase your bet size and spend all your profits. Any serious losing streak will kill you when you are betting too high a percentage of your "real" bankroll.

Constant fluctuations in the amount bet are also killing because you wind up betting the smaller amounts on your winning streaks and larger amounts on your losing streaks. Increasing your bet size after losing periods doesn't work because sometimes betting techniques go sour, particularly when the competition determines the odds, as in horse racing.

I can hear the handicappers out there saying, "But what about the super bet, the special situation when you know you have a big edge?" If you are a handicapper and have varying degrees of confidence in your bets, bankroll the different levels separately. Have a bankroll for your great bets, good bets, and so-so bets. No bet is ever so good you should risk more than five percent of your "real" bankroll.

If your financial situation is such that you can't afford a bankroll that will permit you to make enough money to make it all worthwhile, then just gamble for fun and for small amounts until you have a decent bankroll. If you try to make a bundle on a small investment, you must be extraordinarily lucky to succeed.

If you don't have the bankroll but you want to give one or more of the techniques in this book a whirl, try getting some investors. Let them read the book, and, if they are convinced that you can handle it, they put up the money, you do the work. They get 75 percent of the profits; you get 25 percent. That's my standard deal for investors now. If you follow the techniques exactly and use the money management formulas exactly, it will be a good deal for them and a good deal for you.

If you have the money but not the time, find yourself a smart fellow with the time, and put up the money and let him do the work. I have done that whenever I couldn't devote the time, and it has worked out very well.

You now have all the information you need to be a winner. You can beat the competition, if you want to. The next chapter is devoted to the development of a winning attitude, wanting to win and knowing how to tell when you are gambling to lose or just for the sake of action. If you truly gamble to win, you will. If you gamble for any other reason, you will lose. It really is that simple.

14 | The Winning Psychology

You know one of the surest ways to tell a winner from a loser? Ask a person why he bet the amount he bet and the way he bet, before and after the bet has been decided. The winning gambler has the same answer before and after, whether he wins or loses. The losers know better after. They should have bet more when they won, less, or even not at all—or the opposite, when they lose. The loser becomes smarter when the bet has been decided. "I should have," are the most commonly uttered words from losers.

The winners will tell you they made the right bet, for the right amount, win or lose. Why? Because they have bet according to a plan, following their own rules for what constitutes a good bet. Second-guessing is not a winning habit. No one pays off on what you "should have" done. You have to get it right the first time around.

So, the first prerequisite of the winning psychology is to bet according to a plan. A plan is very simple. It involves only two elements. How much to bet and what bets to make. If your plan is good, it will make money. If it is bad, you will lose money. You will know whether your plan is good or bad by the results. You keep the good plans, get rid of, or improve, the bad plans. If you gamble without a plan, you won't know what you did right when you win, or what you did wrong when you lose. But most important of all, when you don't have a plan, you can become your own worst enemy and make bad bets just because you are, for whatever reason, in a losing frame of mind. All of us have some "winner" in us, and some "loser." Having a set of rules to follow in the form of a plan protects our winning side from our losing side.

The second step in developing the winning psychology is to set realistic goals. Don't expect miracles. Don't expect to get incredibly lucky. A 10-percent edge in any game is enormous. If you plan on the basis of more than that, you are going to be disappointed more often than not. Don't expect to win every bet. Very good bets lose all the time.

The bettor with a winning edge has the law of averages on his side, if he gives it a chance to operate. If you think you can't lose, you will overbet and risk going broke before the odds have had a chance to even up. Aiming too high causes many gamblers to tamper with winning techniques and turns them into losers. If you set reasonable goals, understand that you can lose in the short run, and have the patience to wear down the competition, you will come out on top in the end. If you are in a hurry, you have to be lucky to be a winner. Never count on luck. Count on your winning edge.

The next thing you must do is know when money is yours and when it isn't. How often have you heard someone justify a whopping bet by saying they were playing with the bookie's or the casino's money? That's silly. If it belonged to the bookie, you couldn't bet with it. If you have it, it is *yours.* Why give it back? I assure you, no bookie in the world views the money you lose as *your* money. Once they get it, they keep it. This is cardinal sin number one of the loser, viewing his winnings as money to lose. Personally, I like spending what I win.

On the other hand, once you lose money, it isn't yours anymore. But you constantly hear people say, "I gotta win *my* money back," which is usually tantamount to saying they are about to lose the money that is theirs trying to chase those lost bucks.

"Your" money is the money you have. "Their" money is all the rest of the money in the world. If you understand that, you will save yourself the price of this book hundreds of times during the rest of your life.

Another important ingredient in the winning psychology is to learn to give in a little to your weaknesses, but very little. All gamblers gamble for fun as well as money. The secret is to know when you are making a bet just for fun. If you know this, you can keep the amount down around the price you are willing to pay for the amount of entertainment you will get in return. For example, if a Monday night football game is worth about as much as a movie to me (in terms of total enjoyment) and a movie costs four bucks, then I can bet eighty bucks as an amusement bet. I figure to lose an average of four bucks on random picks over the long run, so it is a reasonable amount to bet.

If you say an eighty-dollar bet won't make the game interesting enough, then maybe you don't like football and you should go to a movie. If you bet serious money just for entertainment, you won't have anything left to bet for fun *and* profit. To be a winner, you must be able to differentiate between the fun bet and the winning bet.

Finally, winning is not a matter of luck. You win because you are making good bets. You lose because you are making bad bets. I lose at poker because I am a bad poker player, not an unlucky one. I win at baseball because I am a good baseball bettor, not a lucky one. The more you blame luck, the longer you will be a loser. Luck is important in the short run. Skill is important in the long run.

I don't deny the existence of luck. A large number of events are determined by luck. The saying "I'd rather be lucky than good" makes a lot of sense. But I don't know how you go about being lucky, so that leaves me no choice but to try and be good. If you want to be a winner, rely on skill, not luck. If you are a loser, you can change your skill, but you are stuck with your luck.

Here is a list that I use to make sure I am not falling back into my old losing habits. I check this list every time I hit a bad streak just to make sure the loser in me hasn't gotten the upper hand.

1. Am I betting more than I can afford?
2. Am I betting to "show" somebody?
3. Am I making today the most important day or this week the most important week?
4. Am I ignoring my plan and breaking rules?
5. Am I making more bets than I usually do, just for the action?
6. Am I chasing lost money?
7. Do I feel like I'm so far ahead it's all right if I lose some?
8. Am I betting hunches or expecting to get lucky?
9. Am I doing a lot of dreaming about striking it rich?
10. Am I getting lazy about keeping records?
11. Do I have the feeling that I'd like to get something over and done with?
12. Am I feeling good about losing?
13. Do I feel like a loser?
14. Am I getting greedy?
15. Am I in a bad streak or making bad bets?
16. Was I feeling invulnerable when the streak started?
17. Have I been overrating some single fact?
18. Am I making "heart" bets?

I am amazed at how often I get affirmative answers to some of those questions. I know better, but the losing attitudes are so powerful, they sneak out at every opportunity. It is a constant struggle to maintain a winning psychology. I hope it is an easier fight for you and that you win the battle.

I've told you most of my sports-betting secrets, except a few that require the use of a computer, and a few that are too new for me to be sure they work. Not all of the things in this book are going to continue working. Most of them will. That's gambling. Things change, and you must change with them. I know some of you will make thousands of times the cost of this book using my secrets because I have. I know some of you will lose because that's what you want to do. But if you follow all the advice in this book, you will be a winner. I have enjoyed writing this book, and I hope you have enjoyed reading it. Maybe someday we will bump into each other in the cashier's line, collecting our winnings together.

Index

Ainslie, Tom, 160
Allen, George, 106
Anxiety, need for, 153–54

Baltimore Colts, 105, 106, 112
Baseball:
  computer simulation program, 32–33
  handicapping, *see* Baseball handicapping
  home-team advantage in, 34, 52
  newspaper accounts of games, 52
  predictable (predictive) statistics in, 34–35
Baseball betting, 170
  betting public in, 27
  bookie's take (house percentage) in, 25–26
  chances of beating the game, 31–32
  competition in, 26–27
  conversion formula for, 35
  honesty of the game and, 27–28, 32
  information available for, 28–29, 32
  injuries approach, 78
  liking the game and, 29–31
  non-system techniques for, 75–78
  odds in, 24–25, 35
  rookie pitchers approach, 77–78
  rules of, 24–25, 32
  special abilities of bettor and, 31
  "ten worst pitchers in baseball" approach, 75–77
Baseball betting system, 36–71
  advantages and disadvantages of, 36
  average number of runs per game, for both leagues, 41–42
  bullpen rating, 38–39, 44–45, 56, 57, 67–68

change of teams by pitchers, 39–40, 45–47

converting run difference to a line, 51, 58–59

daily routine, 51–71

determining if a game is bettable, 52, 57, 60–61

home-team advantage adjustment, 52

money management techniques for, 182–83

offensive rating of teams, 40–41, 49–50, 56–57, 62, 67

personal experiences of author with, 72–75

pitchers' ratings, 39, 47–49, 51–53, 61–62, 69–70

predicting number of runs, 51, 57, 58, 69–71

profit rate from, 57–58

starting a season, 37–50

unearned-run percentage, 38, 42–43, 56, 57, 68–69

watching and listening to games, 52

Baseball handicapping, 37, 78–88

batting order and, 79–82

drawbacks to, 86–88

managers and, 79–84

pitchers and, 83–86

Baseball managers, 79–84

Baseball parks, adjustment factors for, 46–47

Baseball players:

injuries to, 29, 52

intangibles of, 33

key, 86

offensive rating of, 40–41, 49–50, 56

See also Batting order; Pitchers

Basketball, 170

Batting average, 34

Batting order, 79–82

stability of, 79

Blackjack, 175–76, 181

Bookies:

legal, 147–49

illegal, 175

Bookie's take (house percentage):

in baseball, 25–26

in football, 90–91

Bowling, 170, 176–77

Buffalo Bills, 106–7, 111

Bullpen rating, 38–39, 44–45, 56, 57, 67–68

Bunts, 83

Calculator, electronic, 38

Card games, 181

See also Blackjack

Casino gambling, 171–72

Chess, 178

Chicago Bears, 114, 116, 117, 119–22

Cincinnati Bengals, 105–6, 111–12

Cold Sheet, The (magazine), 92

College football, 130–31, 170

Competition:

in baseball betting, 26–27

in football betting, 91

winning approach and, 174–75

Computer, 171, 172, 178

baseball conversion formula derived by using, 35

Computer simulation program, 32–33
Cornerbacks, 125–26

Dallas Cowboys:
  defensive style of, 102–4, 114
  offensive style of, 102, 103, 108–9
  philosophy of, 101–4
Disciplinary benchings (baseball), 29
Dreamers, 154–56

Earned-run average (ERA), 34
  change of teams and, 40, 45–47
  unearned-run percentage used to adjust, 38, 43
Economy, betting on the, 165
Ego satisfaction, 156
Elson, Bob, 30
Emotional gamblers, 156
Execution, games of, 175–77

Football betting, 89–146
  bookie's take (house percentage) in, 90–91
  competition in, 91
  honesty of the game and, 91–92
  information available for, 92–93
  injuries and, 92–93, 124, 134
  liking the game and, 93–94
  rules of, 90
  special abilities of bettor in, 94–95

Football betting system, 130–46
  for college football, 130–31, 170
  information needed for, 133
  injuries and, 134
  logic behind, 132–33
  runaway games and, 134
  step-by-step description of, 134–46
  weather and, 133–34
  wins percentage of, 131–32
Football games, watching, 122–23
Football handicapping, 99–129
  current strengths and weaknesses of each team and, 116–29
  defensive styles and, 102–6, 133–41
  illustration of, 127–29
  offensive styles and, 102–6, 108–12
  organization philosophy of teams and, 99–107
Football teams, 95–97
  defensive styles of, 102–6, 113–14
  offensive styles of, 102–6, 108–12
  See also specific teams
Forty-cent line, 24, 25

Gamblers, 150–90
  dreamers, 154–56
  guilt-ridden, 152–53
  need for anxiety of, 153–54
  "personal," 156
  winning, 157–63
  See also Losing psychology; Winning psychology

Gambling:
  on the economy, 165
  institutional, 166–67
  head-to-head, 166
  on tangibles, 165, 170–71
Gambling opportunities, 164–73
  enjoyment and, 168
  financial position and, 168–69
  talents of bettor and, 167
  temperament and, 169
  types of, 165–67
Gambling school, 171–73
Gambling Times (magazine), 92
Green Bay Packers, 109–10
Guards, offensive, 124–25
Guilt, 152–53

Hackett, Buddy, 153
Handicapping (intuitive betting), *see* Baseball handicapping; Football handicapping
Harness races, 170
Head-to-head gambling, 166
Home runs, 34
Home-team advantage:
  in baseball, 34, 52
  in football, 132
Horse racing, 18, 19, 160–61, 169–70
  money management and, 183

IBM 360/65, 33
Information, 172
  baseball betting and, 28–29, 32

football betting and, 92–93, 133
  winning approach and, 175
Injuries:
  in baseball, 29, 52, 78
  in football, 92–93, 124, 134
Institutional gambling, 166–67
Intuitive betting, *see* Baseball handicapping; Football handicapping
Isaacs, Neil, 92

Kicking teams, 122–23
Knox, Chuck, 106–7
Kramer, Jerry, 100

Las Vegas, 147–49, 172
Legislation, 172
Linebackers, 125
Linemakers, professional:
  in baseball betting, 26, 27
  in football betting, 91, 93
Line play (football), 123–24
Lineup, *see* Batting order
Los Angeles Rams, 102, 114
  philosophy of, 103
Losing psychology, 19, 21, 150–58, 189
Luck, 188–89

Managers, baseball, 79–84
Minnesota Vikings, 102, 110–11, 114
  philosophy of, 103
Money management, 20–21
Money management system, 180–85

Nevada, 147–49
New England Patriots, 105
New York Jets, 116, 117, 120–21

Oakland Raiders, 102, 111–12, 114, 116–19
  philosophy of, 103–4
Odds:
  in baseball betting, 24–25, 35
  in football betting, 90
  on a random bet winning, 174
Over and under bets:
  in baseball, 25
  in football, 90

Parlay cards, 90
Parlays, 90, 91
"Personal" gamblers, 156
Pitchers (starting pitchers):
  change of teams, 39–40, 45–47
  earned-run average (ERA) of, *see* Earned-run average
  handicapping and, 83–86
  managers' change of, 83
  non-system technique involving rookies, 77–78
  relief, *see* Relief pitchers
  "ten worst pitchers in baseball" approach, 75–77
  total defensive rating for, 39, 47–49, 51–53, 61–62, 69–70
  updating rating of, 53, 61–62
"Pitchers must go" specification, 24–25
Pittsburgh Steelers, 104–5
Point spread, 90
Poker, 19–20

Predictable (predictive) statistics in baseball, 34–35
  See also specific statistics
Prediction, games of, 177–79
Predictive variables, 177–79
Pro Bowl, 122
Pro Football News, 92
"Proposition" bets, 148
Psychology, *see* Losing psychology; Winning psychology
Punt returns, 123

Quarterbacks, 126

Relief pitchers, 34
  bullpen rating of, 38–39, 44–45, 56, 57, 67–68
Religion, 150
Rookies (baseball), 40–41
Rules:
  of baseball betting, 24–25, 32
  of football betting, 90
  winning approach and, 174
Run line in baseball betting, 24
Runs:
  average number of, per game, for both leagues, 38, 41–42
  number of, 51, 57, 58, 69–71
Runs batted in per plate appearance, 34
Runs scored per plate appearance, 34

Sacrifices (bunts), 83
St. Louis Sporting News, 28

School, gambling, 171–73
Self-punishment, 152
Simulation program, 32–33
Sporting News, The, 37, 41
Sports Form (magazine), 92
Strine, Gerald, 92

Tackles, defensive, 124
Take sign, 83
Talents of bettor:
    in baseball betting, 31
    in football betting, 94–95
    gambling opportunities and, 167
Tangibles, gambling on, 165, 170–71, 181, 182
Teasers, 90, 91
Ten-cent line, 24, 25
Twenty-cent line, 24, 25

Unearned-run percentage, 38, 42–43, 56, 57, 68–69
Unearned runs, 34

Variables, predictive, 177–79

Walk, intentional, 83
Washington Redskins, 106
Weather:
    in baseball betting, 29
    in football betting, 133–34
Who's Who of Baseball, 37
Winning approach, 174–85
    to games of execution, 175–77
    to games of prediction, 177–79
    money management system and, 180–85
Winning psychology, 157–63, 186–90